# GRANDPA
*Tell Us A Story*

*Jay Bullock*

**GRANDPA: TELL US A STORY**
Published by Grandpa's House
Wrens, Georgia

Copyright © 2022 by Jay Bullock. All rights reserved.

No part of this book may be reproduced in any form or by any mechanical means, including information storage and retrieval systems, without permission in writing from the publisher/author, except by a reviewer who may quote passages in a review.

All images, logos, quotes, and trademarks included in this book are subject to use according to trademark and coypright laws of the United States of America.

ISBN: 979-8-9854315-1-3
BIOGRAPHY & AUTOBIOGRAPHY / Personal Memoirs

Editorial services provided by Joyce Beverly, MyStoryographer.com
Cover and interior design by Kate Walker, Circle Creative

All rights reserved by Jay Bullock and Grandpa's House

Printed in the United States of America

JAY BULLOCK

*For my Grands*

# Introduction

## *My Dearest Grandchildren*

I spend a lot of time thinking of what I would give to you. I love to give you gifts, to see you smile. To experience joys of life together with you is the ultimate reward. When Makenzie was just a wee toddler, I'd push her in a swing in front of Jay's Hardware and she'd laugh and I'd exclaim, "Wee willigers!" It was just a crazy name from the imagination of my mind. Very similar to names I'd call my dogs when I was nine years old and imagination was wild and uninhibited.

To watch Titus Jay dress up as a cowboy or a policeman or whatever else is just pure beauty and inspiring. Kelby's eyes lighting up just before his dad stomps the gas pedal on the Razor and scares Grandpa out of his wits, portrays the hope and energy of the youngest Bullock generation.

Listening to Alexia exclaiming "what I think is" in her grownup vocabulary at six years old is both hilarious and exhilarating. To see her persona develop – what will the years hold?

Dillan takes on the world with no fear. Grandparents marvel at his zeal and courage wondering what's next, and when, not if. Hudson Dean, our miniature Jeremy, who at three years old seeks to understand all he can. Where will life take you Hudson? Or rather, where will you take it? The curly haired Liam Blake, shadowing big brother, portraying a work ethic and willingness to help whatever the task at hand regardless of the fact you have only been on this earth for two years.

Somewhere over the rainbow my grandson I never met, Sawyer Diesel I imagine on a cloud floating blissfully here and there. One can only imagine. My dear friend Jenny Kay says she thinks we come from Heaven and if we choose right and live for Jesus we go back to Heaven. Could it be? For sure I live knowing that Sawyer is playing on those streets of gold and meadows so fair. Let's meet him there!

There have been lots of gifts. Grandma will spend whatever if she thinks the grands will enjoy. And why not? What else brings so much joy? But the best of gifts are short lived. Some seasonal, others answer a period of life, trends that fade swiftly like hoverboards! I think of words I heard at Bible school, "...what will I give him, I'll give him my heart!"

My heart, 'tis what I'd like to give to you, my very dear Grands. You will need no inheritance, you can create all that you need if you follow your parents and your grandparents and yeah even great grands. The lessons available to launch and drive you hold value beyond dollars and cents. They are the key to true success, joy, prosperity, and happiness.

The stories in this book hold many of the lessons I have learned over the years. It is my joy to share them with you in hopes you will smile and grow wise.

*With all my love, Grandpa*

# Table of Contents

Rodney & Mona Rabun ..................................................... 1
Trooper Terry ................................................................ 3
Mac & Cheese ............................................................... 5
Rodney At Last! ............................................................. 9
The Basement Project ................................................... 13
The Dune Buggy ........................................................... 17
Car Thief ..................................................................... 19
Chris Ryan .................................................................. 21
Eating Crow ................................................................. 25
The Wish Book ............................................................. 27
Construction Site ......................................................... 31
Going to My Grandparent's House ................................. 33
My Grandmother's House ............................................. 35
Cleaning the House ...................................................... 43
My First Money-Making Scheme ................................... 47
Pizza Hut! .................................................................... 51
Memory ....................................................................... 55
My First Watch ............................................................. 57
Memories of My Grandfather Burt ................................. 59
Granddad Burt's Van .................................................... 61
Mayor Burt .................................................................. 63
My First Trip to the Farm .............................................. 65
Milking Cows ............................................................... 67
Hyatt Place .................................................................. 73
Peer Pressure .............................................................. 79
The Bear Cat ............................................................... 87
The Hog Story ............................................................. 93
The Bear Sighting ........................................................ 101

# 1

## *Rodney & Mona Rabun*

When I was about 11 years old, we moved to 3555 Jonathan Circle in Augusta. It was a new neighborhood called Apple Valley. My mother bought a three-bedroom house at the back of the subdivision. We had a very deep lot that went way back to a ditch. Beyond that ditch were hundreds of acres of woods which became my playground.

I can see right now it's going to take a while to get to the Rodney Rabun part. But that's okay! Sometimes people say, "I digress," which is a fancy term for getting off track on to a different story. But I digress again.

Apple Valley was a nice neighborhood with hundreds of homes. The price range and finance options accommodated retired folks, Army people, young families, and middle-income families. I had a lot of friends there. Keith Perry, John Marshall, David McCoy, Chris Ryan, and many more I can't recall the names of now, 48 years later.

## GRANDPA, TELL US A STORY

Why just the other day, David McCoy stopped by Jay's Ace to see if the Jay of Jay's Ace Hardware was the same one he remembered. I hadn't heard from him since I'd moved away at age 14. Unfortunately, I wasn't there, but we did chat on the phone a little and caught up after all these years.

This was the first house we lived in that was "ours." Not a rent house. I'm sure my Mom had a loan with 30 years of payments to make, but there was still that satisfaction of buying our very own home. We could do whatever we wanted to it.

I had a dog; Snoopy was his name. But I wanted more, lots more. My dear mother had a very large dog kennel pen built for me. I think it was ten feet wide and 40 ft long. She even had a concrete floor poured in for me so the dogs wouldn't get out. I was thrilled beyond words. I added Lucky, a shaggy black dog, a beagle (I can't remember its name), and five – yes five! – more dogs to the mix. There were eight dogs in all.

I had so much fun with those critters. They were my pride and joy. I was up early every morning to feed them and take care of their needs before school. Then I went back to the pen after school to let them run free with me.

We went hunting together, although our targets were mostly songbirds and the occasional rabbit. There weren't a lot of deer then like there are now. I thought meadowlarks were quail! I really was ignorant. I read Field and Stream and tried to recreate all the adventures from those pages. Oh, the dreams of a young person!

Every time I reflect on all those dogs, I am thankful to my mom for all the expense and patience with me. The dog food and vet bills were a lot for a young mother with three kids to raise. I did my best to help out to show my appreciation for all she did for me. Looking back, I sure could have done better.

I think we should have called this the dog story!

*Good night! Or shall we read another one?*
*Grandpa*

# 2

## *Trooper Terry*

So, to pay for the new house and all the dog food, my dear mother had to work very hard. Her job was from three in the afternoon to eleven at night. Back in those days, it wasn't as easy for a lady to get a job as it is today. The main jobs a lady could do was be a secretary or a waitress. Today, ladies do nearly all the jobs men do and get almost the same pay.

When we got off the bus after school, Mom was already off to work. My two sisters Beth, age nine, and Jerri Lynn, six, and I had the house to ourselves. It was my job to fix supper for us and make sure we all went to bed on time. Oh, and clean the house.

But there'd be time for all that later on! We hit the ground running.

I, of course, went straight to my dogs. I have no idea what my sisters did. It was probably my job to keep an eye on them, but I was a typical head-strong 11-year-old boy. It's a miracle we all lived through that!

I do remember we watched a lot of TV. At 4:30, Trooper Terry came on. It was a live show where groups of kids came for a birthday party. Trooper Terry was dressed up like a police officer, even though I don't think he was one. And you know how kids are intrigued with police officers.

I don't remember what all they did for the 30 minutes the show lasted. I think each kid was introduced, and this was your big moment to be a star. So, we anxiously watched to see if, by chance, anyone we knew was on there.

The funniest thing I remember was when, all at once, one of the kids was giggling like kids are prone to do. Trooper Terry says to the little girl, "What's so funny?" Right there on Channel 6 public TV, the little girl just says for all the world to hear, "Leroy farted!"

Of course, all the other little kids did just what you are doing now, and they laughed too!

Now I remember Trooper Terry played a cartoon show that the kids and Trooper Terry watched while we watched them watching the cartoon, and we all laughed together. Them on TV and us in our living room watching TV. It seems kind of corny now, but when I see the videos that six to twelve-year old's watch now, maybe it wasn't so different?

Story number two, and I think we are getting farther instead of closer to the Rodney Rabun story!

*Good night! Love y'all!*
*Grandpa*

# 3

## *Mac & Cheese*

After Trooper Terry was over, then The Addams Family came on. It was a funny show about this very weird family who lived in a castle-like house. There was a great big tall guy called the Lurch. He spoke in a real deep voice with always the same expression and tone. There was a girl, probably about 12, named Wednesday Addams. She got into a lot of mischief with her little brother, Pugsley.

The parents were Gomez and Morticia Addams, who looked like a cross between an Italian mobster and a scary movie character. They both had a peculiar charm and a dry sense of humor. The weirdest thing on the show was the Thing, which was just a human hand that stuck out of a box that sat on the counter or the table. As I remember it, Thing had a voice and would offer its own point of view and opinions at just the right time. Now, this is a 48-year-old memory, so it may not be exactly correct.

You see, we tend to remember what we want to and what impresses us a lot. For example, if all eight or nine of us heard and saw the same thing today then were asked about it in five years, we might have eight or nine different stories! But that's ok. It keeps life interesting! Oh, and we'd all think we were right!

After our daily dose of cartoons and entertainment, it was back out the door to get in as much playtime as possible before supper. The target supper time was 6:30, and it seems like reality was more like 7:00 to 7:30. I was the cook, and this was long before every house had a microwave. For that matter, there wasn't even such a thing as a microwave then. My life would have been lots easier if there was!

What we did have was TV dinners, and they came in a multiple choice of menus: turkey and dressing, chicken pot pie, and meatloaf, which only faintly tasted like the real thing, to name a few. Salisbury Steak was my favorite. Don't let the word steak fool you here. It was more like a flat hamburger patty in brown gravy. Google says the price of a TV dinner was originally $1.19 but finally settled to $.59 so more people would buy them.

They came in a tray with three compartments covered in a foil-like wrap. The directions for how to cook them were printed on the top. I remember always reading the directions each time which seems crazy as they probably were all the same. The funny thing is that this is still how I cook today. So, I guess the way you learn something when you are little is how you'll do things when you get old! Be careful what you learn or what you don't learn!

My sisters loved macaroni and cheese, which is probably the all-time number one kids' food ever. We used to own the Dutch House Restaurant, and it seemed like nearly every kid (and lots of grown-up kids) that came through the line wanted mac and cheese. Now *that* mac and cheese was a WHOLE lot different than the mac and cheese we poured out of a box as kids.

The mac and cheese we had as kids started as a box of dry macaroni and a bag of cheese. I don't remember exactly, but we probably added water or milk or whatever we had to the cheese powder and stirred it into the boiling water the macaroni was swimming in.

What I do remember very vividly is my sisters were so hungry, probably because it was now 7:30 or 8:00 o'clock, that they didn't always mix it up very good. So, what you ended up with was the cheap chewy macaroni with this powdery half-mixed cheese sauce on it. I think Beth was always the mac & cheese cook. I hated this not thoroughly mixed concoction, and it still grosses me out nearly five decades later. The ONLY food I don't care for is and has always been mac & cheese!

I've tried it a dozen times over the years but never changed my mind. Well, except for Becky Summy's mac & cheese, which is, of course, well mixed up and made from scratch, which means it ain't come out of a $.99 box!

Who knew I'd tell a story about mac & cheese? Will we ever get to Rodney Rabun? Maybe in a story or two!

*Goodnight!*
*Grandpa*

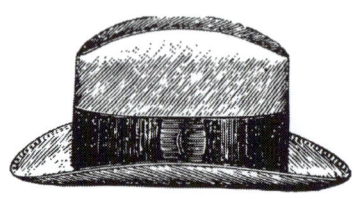

*I think sometimes, when you have a dream, God knows your dream. He wants to help you. He makes things work for you. I don't think that. I know that. He's made a lot of dreams work for me in life.*

# 4

## *Rodney at Last!*

Now, where were we? Oh yes, suppertime. How could I forget, especially when it comes to one of my favorite things, food!

One last word on our suppers, at least for now. Part of the reason they are called TV dinners is they came out about the time TV became popular. Of course, TV endeavors to be interesting and draw people to watch it. I told you about the after-school program we watched. A show for teenagers came on next, followed by the six pm news. Seven o'clock brought shows to capture the family's attention, like game shows or action shows such as Emergency 911 or FBI-type shows.

So along comes a meal you can heat up then eat in the tray it comes in while sitting in front of the TV. You can simply place it on a TV tray and violà, you can eat your supper and not miss your show. I am happy to now live my life without TV and all its distractions! It is much nicer to enjoy meals with those we love and not eat out of a tray.

Again, I digressed. What's new?

The TV was our babysitter for the evening, especially for the months with shorter days like November through February. The other months of spring and summer, we devoured our food and were back out the door. Again, I have no idea where my sisters went. I kind of remember being in the yard or at a neighbor's place trying to keep an eye on where my sisters were.

This is where Rodney Rabun comes in. At last, we may get there!

Rodney and his wife Mona lived across the street from us, kind of catty-corner to our house. Not straight across, but maybe one house up. I'm not sure how we first met, but I can imagine Rodney was out working in his yard, maybe planting grass or watering the newly planted grass.

Rodney was probably 23 years old, but to a curious, adventuresome 11-year-old, he seemed like an older mature guy. He became a real mentor and influence in my life.

Mona was a typical young bride with a two-year-old daughter, Michelle. They never had any other children. Michelle would become like a little sister to me.

I would come to spend many hours in this home. Faintly now, I recall my mother screaming at me about spending too much time over there. Her admonitions and screams went in one ear and out the other, as they say.

I think Rodney always hoped to have a son, and I began to take on that role. He became a very strong and good influence in my young life. I often think of how the things he taught me come back to me so many times.

I believe God put Rodney and Mona in my life to keep me out of trouble and help me become the person I am. I know to you as grandchildren you probably only think of me as old Grandpa. But somewhere inside is this little boy still trying to get out. Believe it or not, many years ago, I was a little kid or young person just like you except without a dad there at home like you have.

Dear Father in Heaven,

Thank you for my Mom and Dad, who love and care for me, who feed me and buy me clothes and nice things. Most of all, thank you for being in their hearts, so they live for you, God! Amen.

*Goodnight!*
*Grandpa*

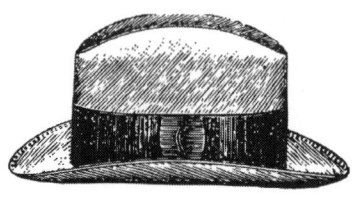

*Sometimes people don't think much of your ideas. It can be kind of embarrassing to go ahead and do them. It kind of gets back into peer pressure, but you got to remember, if you have a vision, you have a dream, follow that dream.*

# 5

## *The Basement Project*

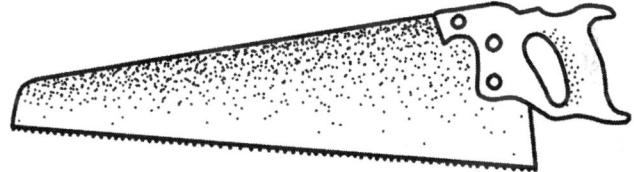

Now, you didn't think I brought you this far just to tell you one Rodney story, did you? No siree, buddy, there's more to come.

So, Rodney and Mona had a two-story house with a basement. The basement was unfinished, just walls of studs exposed. Sometimes they build a house like this and don't finish the basement so they can sell it for less, and then the homeowners can finish it out later. If they are a handyman like Rodney was, they can often save some money. Also, when they buy the home, they don't have to have as much money upfront. When they finish it out, they can do so as they have extra money. This was my friend Rodney's plan.

Rodney worked for the telephone company. This was back way before cell phones. There were actual telephones on the wall or on the counter with a cord hooked to the wall. The plug on the wall was hooked to a wire that ran to the outside. There was a connection box on the outside of the house with a wire that went overhead or underground to a metal podium or post that hooked up to another wire that ran miles and miles to a central switchboard somewhere.

Rodney's job was to go out and fix the wires when they were broken or had a bad connection. It was a fairly technical job, and he enjoyed it. He drove a telephone company van; I believe it was Bell South?

Mona worked as a receptionist at a dentist's office. Remember how I told you earlier that back then ladies were either secretaries or waitresses? Well, a receptionist is like a secretary for a doctor or dentist. Michelle went to daycare.

Rodney got off work around 4:00, so he had a long afternoon. This worked out great for me to drop by his place after the aforementioned TV shows and the dogs were fed.

One of the first projects I helped him with was the basement walls. Back then, paneling was all the rage. It was simple to install; the sheets of paneling were 4 ft. wide and 8 ft. long. Most walls are 8 ft. tall, so you could just stand up the paneling and nail it to the studs. Seems simple enough, but always remember nothing is quite as simple as it looks. First of all, the studs had to be in the right places so the 4 ft. wide part matches up. If there were receptacles (plug-ins) or light switches on the wall, you needed to cut the paneling to go over those. Otherwise, you might cover up your plug-ins! And that's not so smart!

Of course, all this seems simple enough, but I had never done it before. So I had lots of questions for Rodney as we worked together. He patiently answered them all for me and taught me a lot of practical things I still use today.

The first thing we had to do was to go buy the paneling. There were not a lot of stores back then like there are now. We went to

Sears to get paint and tools and nails. I think we got the paneling from a lumber place.

The exciting part is Rodney asked me to go with him! This was a real treat to me as most of my life was spent with my Mom and sisters and my mom's friends, who were, of course, mostly ladies too. So, it was really cool to be able to ride with Rodney for a couple of hours and do some guy things. I'm sure I riddled him with dozens and probably hundreds of questions as we rode together. I remember him saying, "Boy, you have lots of questions!" I still do. That's how you learn stuff. I tried my best to help out with the loading and later on unloading at the house.

Of course, once we were home and ready to work, there was always something we'd forgotten or didn't anticipate needing. So back to the store again! Most of these trips were on Saturday morning when I didn't have to watch my sisters, so don't think I forgot them! (Well, there were times I did forget them, I'm sure!)

*Good night! I'll tell you more another day.*
*Grandpa*

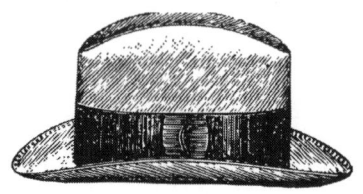

*Have the courage to follow your dreams and ideas. You never know what they might do for you.*

# 6

## *The Dune Buggy*

So, my first real carpenter experience was in that basement of Rodney's home. I would try to hold the paneling in place while Rodney nailed it. I'm sure I saved Mona a lot of stress, but I probably was a lot of stress to Rodney. If questions would have held the paneling in place, it would have been anchored to the walls forever!

We would work for a while then go upstairs for a glass of tea and a snack. I have no idea what we ate or drank, really, but I do remember Rodney was very good about taking a break every so often. Probably hoping I would leave!

After a busy morning one day, he said, "Let's go ride in the dune buggy." Of course, I was excited! About as excited as Kelby taking Grandpa for a ride on the Razor!

We tooled down the road toward the lock and dam about three miles. Rodney found some really neat and steep hills to explore. I was not ready for what happened next! We went nearly straight up a very tall steep incline. I thought at any moment we'd flip over backward. Close to the top, the dune buggy refused to go on, and suddenly we rolled back down way faster than we went up!

Later at supper, he told Mona he too thought we were going to flip! Lots of comfort that was to me!

And you know what? We went back again and again. We finally conquered that hill but not without a few more scary rollbacks. I guess that's why they call it an adventure!

Would you like to try that? What's the scariest ride you have ever been on?

*Good night! Sweet dreams!*
*Grandpa*

# 7

## *Car Thief*

Not long after we moved into Apple Valley, my mom bought a new car. It was a Ford. She had the car for about four months.

One Saturday morning, around 8:30, a man knocked on our door. He said he was from the Ford place and could he get the keys to the car to take it in for a service checkup. I think he may have first asked for my mother, and I told him she was sleeping.

I tiptoed to her room and got the keys off her dresser, tiptoed back out of the room, and gave them to the Ford guy. I felt good that I had been so helpful. Little did I know...

Later in the morning, Mom woke up and said we were going to go shopping.

"How is that?" I asked.

"In the car, silly," she said.

I told her very proudly, I didn't think so, since the Ford place had her car.

"What are you saying?" she asked.

I explained how I'd been so helpful. She did not seem happy or impressed.

She called the Ford place, and no, they had not sent anyone out. Oh no! Apparently, we had been scammed by a car thief. My Mom was NOT happy. After a long screaming session directed to me and a clear understanding, I learned a valuable lesson.

We called the police, and they came out and asked me lots of questions, like "Did I know the guy?" "How old was he?" "How tall was he?" Then they wrote their report.

Mom eventually calmed down. The insurance paid for the stolen car, and we got another new car.

But that's not the end of the story! Six months later, I went outside one Sunday morning and walked to my friend Chris Ryan's house. Of course, I walked. I walked everywhere I went or rode my bike.

Just as I turned the corner onto the cul-de-sac where he lived, there in front of me was the car! It was very dirty and dinged up, with a few small dents, but it was the same blue car I gave away.

I ran home as fast as I could to tell my Mother the car had been returned. Just like the guy said he would, he'd brought it back. Of course, it was well used and had been driven a lot of miles. Again, the police came and checked it out. I think they took it with them.

In a few days, they caught the guy and put him in jail. Later on, I had to go to court and tell the judge what had happened. That was scary and exciting at the same time!

The lesson of this story is to be careful what people tell you. Don't listen to strangers. It's ok to wake up your Mom or Dad if something important comes up. There are some bad people out there. Be careful!

*Good night. Sweet dreams!*
*Grandpa*

# 8

## Chris Ryan

Chris was one of my best friends when I was growing up. He lived just around the corner from me on Jonathan Circle. He actually lived back in a cul-de-sac. I didn't know what a cul-de-sac was back then. I learned later on, it's kind of where a street goes back in and makes a little loop and comes back out, and they build houses around the loop. They can get more houses packed in some lots, I think, which is partly why they do it that way.

Do you know anybody who lives in a cul-de-sac? I know my good friend, Brian Lewis, now he lives in one. I think it's really cool. Just how they sit back, kind of a quiet and off the street.

Chris lived in a cul-de-sac just around the corner from me. It was probably, I don't know, six or seven houses down. I can see it very clearly in my mind right now. I would walk probably about, I don't know, 500 to 800 feet, and then I turned right and walk about that far again. His house was in the back, kind of. I told you earlier, we had a really deep lot. Their lot would've been a lot shallower and smaller.

Chris's mother was a lot older than my mom. My mother, at that point in her life, was probably 31 years old, maybe 32, and Chris's mom would've been about 50, it seemed like. She must have been a lot older when he was born.

Of course, I was younger. So she was probably 40 something and just seemed older. I do remember she had a boyfriend, that she didn't have a husband, and he was 60, it seemed like, or older. Again, he might not have been that old, but it just seemed that way. I remember Chris saying how old he was.

Seems like Chris maybe had a sister. I can't remember, for sure. But he had a lot of free time on his hands. He could go and do whatever he wanted to do. His mother was working a lot, and Chris was probably not the best influence to be with. But we had similar interests in hunting and running around through the woods and riding bikes and blowing firecrackers up, and stuff like that. So we spent a lot of time together.

So, Chris and I, one of the things we did together that was a lot of fun, we camped out at night, and it was easy for him to do. I think sometimes his mother didn't even come home at night. That's why I'm about sure he had older sister and she didn't really care what he did.

And so he and I camped out. It wasn't that far from our houses, back in the woods, just straight back behind our house. But when you're 12 or 13 years old, camping out is a lot of fun to do. It doesn't matter how far away you are. We had a little pop up tent and we had all our stuff out there. Each one of us probably had a flashlight. Flashlights weren't near as nice back then as they are today. Today, there's really cool lights you go camping with.

I remember that it got cold and we got hungry late at night. I remember about midnight, boy we were hungry. We thought we'd cook something on a campfire, but we didn't have anything to cook.

Chris said, "Hey, my mother just bought some meat and has it all in the freezer." So we slipped in his house and looked and sure enough, there was all kinds of packs of meat. We got some hot dogs out of there, and I don't know what else, but we went out there and made us a fire, and we cooked those hot dogs. And best I can remember, they were really, really good.

I know numerous times we'd go raid that freezer and get whatever we wanted to cook out. I do remember finally, one day his mother all at once looking in that freezer, and a lot of her stuff was gone, and she was not happy with us. She gave him a real chewing out, and I think he might have got in a lot more trouble than that. For a long time, we weren't allowed to get anything from his house to eat.

I guess the moral of this story is: make sure and ask your parents before you go taking food out of the house. That way they know, especially if you're getting as much food out of the house as we got.

But that wasn't Chris's style. And I remember, later on he went on like nothing ever happened.

That's probably not a good way to be. We should be a lot more obedient and respectful of people. And especially our parents.

*Okay, good night!*
*Grandpa*

*You can have all the ideas you want with your life and all the dreams. If you follow somebody else's, you're not going to get where you want to go... You might end up where you don't know to be, so it's best to have your own direction and go where you want to go without somebody else influencing you.*

# 9

## *Eating Crow*

Now there is a saying about eating crow, which means you have been proven wrong about something you said or did. This story however is not about that! It is about my experience eating a real crow. Yes, I know, gross!

So, I mentioned earlier about my many hunting escapades and adventures when I was growing up. At age 11, I would often take off on a Saturday morning into the woods behind my house in Apple Valley in Augusta. Sometimes I'd take a hunting buddy and always a dog or two or three. I had a beagle for rabbits. A coon dog who I only dreamed of coon hunting with. Nope it never happened. And a bird dog, a pointer, who unfortunately never found any real game birds like quail or pheasants.

What we did find was lots of meadowlarks, sparrows, songbirds, and crows. Most of them survived my attempts to take them down with only a BB or pellet gun. Later I progressed to a shotgun, probably at age 13-14 I'm guessing. On this particular excursion, I can't remember the weapon of choice. I do remember getting very hungry and being over three miles from home.

I managed to kill a crow and another much smaller bird. I had planned to spend the entire day in the woods. I brought along my canteen full of water and some matches to build a fire on which to prepare my lunch.

For the first time I plucked the feathers off of the dead crow, remembering all I read in the Field and Stream magazine. I even washed it off with some of my water. I'm sure there were stories about tasty birds like quail and pheasants NOT crows. But hey, when you are 12 and haven't had a dad to train you, best to figure it out on your own. Oops, I digressed again!

I built a small fire with some sticks and leaves, being very careful to not cause a forest fire. Kids, don't try this on your own! Looking back, it was a miracle I didn't cause a real disaster! I constructed a tripod out of bigger sticks and hung my bird over the fire to cook. I don't think I'd ever even cooked on a grill at this point in life. I really had no clue what I was doing.

Of course, being hyper by nature didn't help. I doubt I cooked it anywhere near long enough. But after what seemed like forever and being now very hungry, I began eating my roasted crow. And it was …nasty. I did manage to eat half of it. I was quite hungry; I then tried the other bird. It was a robin, I think. It was a little better.

I never tried this again and I don't recommend that you do so either!

*Goodnight!*
*Grandpa*

# 10

## *The Wish Book*

Sears Roebuck is probably one of the oldest retail shopping places in America. It actually started doing business in 1892!

Somewhere along the way, they dropped the "Roebuck" part of the name and became known as "Sears." They were the Amazon of years ago, and the Lowes or Home Depot and the Target, and well, they had just about everything in one place.

Sears was one of the first merchants to send out catalogs. You could order clothes, toys, appliances, dishes, and even kits to build your own house! As a kid like you, I'd spend hours looking through those pages, dreaming and scheming. As a teenager, I nearly drooled as I poured over the tool section. Me and thousands of others would figure out how much money we needed to make those dreams a reality and go to work saving our coins and bills. My friend Rodney called those "beaners" and "gainers." Gainers were coins, beaners were bills.

I digress again!

Today you can do the same with Amazon, but it is not the same. No matter how fast your internet connection or 5G phone services, it's just not comparable to flipping pages of a catalog. I'm not saying this to be cynical or skeptical. In just a few minutes, you could go from toys to tools to dishes to even live chickens to clothes to washers and dryers.

Once you saved up your beaners, you could send your order in, call them, go to a catalog store in the small rural towns, or, if you lived in a large city, you would be lucky enough to go to an actual Sears store! They were some of the largest stores at the time, and there are still a few left. I just checked, thirty-five left from a peak of three thousand!

Should have kept that catalog, Mr. Roebuck. Somewhere along the way, the catalog was dropped in the interest of progress. When you are in business, you have to be careful what you change.

So in Augusta, we had a Sears store on Walton Way. There was an upstairs with clothing and toys, and downstairs was like a hardware store with appliances, lawnmowers, and big power tools. Finally, I get to my story!

On Saturday morning Rodney would say, "You want to ride to Sears with me?"

Of course I did! I was so excited!

You see, I didn't have my dad to take me places like you do. It felt so special to "ride shotgun" with Rodney. Riding shotgun is an old term that can be like the guard on an armored truck who would be in the passenger seat with a shotgun handy in case of trouble, but later this term "ride shotgun" is just a funny way of saying you are riding in the front passenger seat. Of course, we know how much fussing goes into whose turn it is to ride up front! "Riding shotgun" sounds cooler than "ride up front."

There I am, eleven years old, riding shotgun with my friend Rodney Rabun. I felt pretty important. Rodney taught me how to pick the smooth straight pieces of lumber, choose the best paint color (probably should have asked Mona), what to look for in tools and nails. We'd go early to beat the crowds. I don't even remember there being more people than we have in our Ace Stores!

Sears was a big part of our lives. In early October the Sear's Christmas catalog would arrive. We fought over who got it first. I'd fall asleep going page to page through these six hundred page books. Wish Book is what they were appropriately called.

Do you look at books before you fall asleep? What kind? Or is it is a device like a phone or think pad (Grandpa's word for tablet)?

We'd make our Christmas list complete with page number, item number, and price. I'd read it to my Grandmother on the phone, but most likely, I'd mail it to her. Now Titus sends me links to get it right! The funny thing is I don't remember them ever being out of stuff or any big shortages. We just knew they would have it if we ordered it. In our high-tech world today, not even Amazon does this as well!

*Good night and sweet dreams,*

*Grandpa (who probably learned retail from those Wish Books.)*

*Sometimes if you like something well enough, it doesn't have to make so much money.*

# 11

## *Construction Site*

Behind where we lived in Apple Valley, there was a big construction site. I have no idea what they were building, but I do know there was a lot of big equipment like bulldozers, backhoes, track hoes, and cranes. Now I didn't know the names of the equipment, but I did think it was really cool to slip out there late in the evening after the crew went home and sit in the seats and pretend.

I can't remember if there were fences to keep curious kids and thieves out, but, knowing me and my friends, we probably just figured out how to go over or under. Do you think this was a good idea?

If you said no, you are right! We had no idea what we were doing or the trouble we could cause. I remember we found these big boxes of bolts and nuts. There were probably one-inch nuts and looked like a cool plaything. We pretended they were big rings and put them on each hand. We took bags of them and threw them around like rocks.

Now I am not very proud of this story at all. Rather it is very embarrassing. Every time I talk of it, I feel bad. We were not only stealing but making a lot of trouble for someone to clean up. I tell you this story, so you know what not to do.

If it's not yours, leave it alone. If it is behind a fence and you don't have permission, don't go there. If you don't know what it is, don't mess with it.

What would you do now that you heard this story?

*Goodnight!*
*Grandpa*

# 12

## *Going to My Grandparents' House*

My Grandpa and Grandmother Burt, my mom's parents, lived in Hampton, Virginia. The was about 500 miles from Augusta, Georgia. I think Mom tried to take us there for Christmas or Thanksgiving. I'm not sure if we went every year, but it seemed like it. I know sometimes my grandparents came to visit us. These were very happy times, just like when we are together! I love being with you all. These are some of the happiest times of my life.

When we went to Virginia, it was a road trip. It took about ten hours, but it seemed like it took a lot longer. Isn't that how it is? You are all excited about seeing Grandpa and Grandma, and you can't get there fast enough! Are we there yet? How much longer? Another two hours, really?

We didn't stop for the night at a hotel as that was too expensive. And it was really just a long day's drive, like Oklahoma, which Grandma can drive in a day but not with four kiddos! Or when Preston lived in California, which was three days of driving. Or if

Sawyer Diesel was here, two long days from Colorado. And all that depends on the weather.

Also, the highways are a lot better today, so you can travel faster. There are more restaurants today, like probably 20 times more. There was one more problem. My mother had to go to the bathroom a lot. So my job was to help look for a place with a restroom and help with the map. You see, back then, there were no GPS or cell phones with apps for everything. We used a paper map, and if you got lost, you stopped for directions. This was how we recalculated.

Like me, my mom was scared of bridges. This is probably why I am scared of bridges, too. I can still hear her screaming, "Y'all be quiet! We're on a bridge." This was our clue to quit fighting and hold our breath 'til we crossed the bridge. That was hard! Do you ever fuss and fight when you ride in the car?

No matter what time we arrived at 37 Westover St. Hampton, Virginia, my Grandfather was at the driveway to meet us with a big hug. My mom would always cry, and I'd wonder why. Those were tears of joy and relief.

Are you happy when you get to your grandparents' house? I sure am. I'm glad to have such great grandchildren as each of you is!

*Good night, sweet dreams!*
*Love, Grandpa*

# 13

## *My Grandmother's House*

I wonder what your memories and thoughts are of your grandmother's house. Of course, we all have two grandmothers. How well we know them depends on how old they are and things like that. And sometimes your grandmother can be very, very, very old, and sometimes they can be gone by the time you are old enough to get to know them. I had two grandmothers, a Grandmother Burt, my mother's mother, and I had a Grandmother Rice, my father's mother.

Her name was Grandmother Rice because my Grandpa Bullock got killed in the war on D-day. You probably studied about this at school, or you will. It was a big war. D-day was over in France. The US soldiers attacked from a beach and the German soldiers on the other side were waiting for them. And they were just shooting them as fast as they came on the beach.

My Grandfather Bullock, who would be, oh my goodness, your

great-great-grandfather, he was a medic, an Army doctor. His job was to go on the beach and help the people who had been shot. Of course, technically, they're not supposed to shoot the medics. But you know, when wars are going on, and lots of people are shooting, it's hard to keep from getting shot. And my grandfather got hit while he was helping the wounded men on that beach. He lived about a week and a half before he died from the infection because they were a long way from help. They had to put him on a boat and take him back to the hospital. He laid in the sand for a while, and it was just an awful way to die. Sadly, he didn't make it.

So my grandmother remarried to Paul Rice, who became the only grandfather I knew because my Grandfather Bullock died when my dad was young, long before I was even born. My Grandmother Rice lived in Loveland, Colorado, and my Grandmother Burt lived in Hampton, Virginia. Now I started this story to tell you about my Grandmother Burt's house, and that's what I'm going to tell you about right now. I'm going to stay on topic. I am not going to digress for once.

I spent a lot of time at my grandmother Burt's house for different reasons. At one point, my father was stationed there in Virginia, so we were close by. He was at Langley Air Force Base, even though he was in the Army. It was really handy that we could be right close to my grandmother. We often went there for holidays. After my dad left my mother, my mother would send me to stay with my grandparents for the summer. I think that's because I was a lot of trouble. So it was an easy way to get me out of the way. And that was fine. I had a lot of fun. I never did mind it or feel like I was getting shuffled around or anything. It was fun.

My grandmother's house was at 37 Westover Street, Hampton, Virginia. I didn't have to look that up. I can tell you this from 50 years later because I sent so many letters to them and I memorized that address very early as a young kid. I wonder if you know your grandparents' address. Probably not, because we don't send a lot of stuff in the mail anymore, do we? We pick up a cell phone, we call them, or we video call and we can see them right away. That's so cool. I couldn't do that. All I could do was talk on the phone and imagine what my grandmother looked like. I knew what she looked like, so it was easy to see her. When I talked to her, I had a visual of what I thought she looked like.

Her house was in a nice little neighborhood. I would call it a middle-income neighborhood. Nowadays, it's run down and probably a lower-income neighborhood, but it was a middle-income neighborhood back then. At the upper end of it were some upper-income houses. This house my grandmother had was nice.

In my mind, it was a big house. I went back a few years ago and couldn't believe how much it shrunk! It really didn't shrink. When you're little, everything looks a lot bigger to you. You can imagine if you were only one inch tall, we would look like giants to you then, wouldn't we? That's kind of the way it is when you're little, even though you're not one inch tall.

So this house had two stories. There was not a basement, but there was a downstairs and an upstairs. The upstairs was mostly just a big open area. I was going to say it had two or three bedrooms, but really, thinking back, I remember there being something like curtains or dividers of some kind between the rooms.

I remember my Aunt Denise had a room up there, my Uncle Dennis had a room up there, and I think Mary Lou had a room up there when she was at home. Those were my mom's sisters and brother. She also has another brother, Jimmy, but he was already married and gone when I came along. Dennis and Denise were just a little bit older than I was, nine or 10 years older than me. And so I really looked up to them as a seven or eight-year-old kid. It was fun to hang out with my Uncle Dennis, who was 16 or 17. I had a lot of fun with him. That's a whole 'nother story, though.

The house didn't have any insulation between the floors, but it had a vent, and you could hear everything. If anybody talked downstairs, you heard it upstairs and vice versa. It was a big square vent in the floor in about two places, about three-foot square. It had metal across it, and you could look down and see down below. We would have fun dropping things down through there. My grandpa was like, "Quit dropping stuff down through there!"

My Uncle Dennis would go out and stay out too late at night. When he came home, my grandmother would be waiting for him. She'd chew him out. She fussed and fussed and fussed, and I'd hear every word. I thought, why do you do that every night after she fusses at you like that? But the next night, he'd do it again.

The house had a really nice yard. As a young boy, that yard was my favorite spot. The front yard was fairly small, with a nice fence around it. The fence was about three feet tall, which was just right for a young boy to learn how to jump over the fence. I had a lot of fun learning how to do that. My grandmother often worried I'd get hurt. But I was very small. In school, they called me stick man. I didn't have a belly like I have right now. I was really, really thin. And so I could run and jump, and I had lots of energy. And I'd run and jump over that fence. It was lots of fun. I'd probably grab it with my hands and sling myself over it, something like that. Looking back, it probably wasn't as graceful as it felt.

The backyard was huge, it seemed to me. I remember it had some apple trees in it, and when they were ready, it would be a lot of fun picking apples off those trees. It seems like there were some other fruit trees, but I'm not sure what. There might have been a pear tree. I doubt there was anything else. That's too far north for oranges or things like that. But it does seem like there was a cherry tree.

When I got old enough, part of my job was to cut that grass. That was a lot of fun. It was a big yard to cut, and back then, we didn't have a fancy riding, zero turn mower like I have right now. We didn't have any kind of riding mower. We didn't have any kind of mower with a motor on it.

What we had was a mower that had a reel on it, and you pushed it, and you had to be about nine or 10 to even do this. And if a stick got in, it would just stop right there and throw you up against the handlebars. Boy, it hurt! It made you want to cry. Sometimes I did. That's okay. Things hurt. You can cry. That's right.

So I would mow the grass sometimes, but mostly I played out in the yard. The backyard went off into some woods, much like the house I grew up in that I told you about before.

It was a lot of fun going to other places from there. I could walk down the road from my grandmother's house to a place called Smitty's, which was there until about two years ago when it burned down. I'm hoping they're going to rebuild it back. It was a real cool drive-in hamburger joint, kind of like a Sonic, and locally-owned. They made the best hamburgers and fries.

I would sometimes pick up bottles—you could get a nickel for a bottle—and I would try to find enough bottles, and then I'd turn them in at 7/11, which was a convenience store. When I got a dollar's worth, I could buy myself a Slurpee®. I loved Slurpees®. But again, I digress, which isn't hard for me to do when I think about food. Right now, I'm thinking about food. I'm recording this story as I'm driving to Alexia, Titus, and Liam's house.

Anyhow, so the front porch of the house was really neat. It was kind of like a sunroom-type porch. You walked up to something like a storm door, kind of like a glass screen door, and it would lock. There was a door behind it because the winter was cold there. And then there was a little porch. My grandmother kept a little small organ out on that porch, kind of like a piano. It was a really cool organ. I liked it a lot. She taught me how to play different songs on there. I had a lot of fun sitting beside her, learning how to play that organ.

The main door had a mail slot in it. The mailman would slide the mail through that slot, and it would drop down onto the floor. And then he'd go to the next house. He did this walking from house to house. It was cool when the mail came. It was also cool for little kids like us to peep in and out of that slot, too. Somebody would get on the outside and someone on the inside, and we would look at each other through that slot. That was a lot of fun. I know it sounds really dumb, but it was cool for us kids.

There was a front room, and right off there was a den, and that's where my grandfather would sit. When he came home from work at 4:00, he'd kick back in his recliner and turn the TV on and go straight to sleep. He'd take him a nice little 30-minute or hour-long nap. Then he'd get up and go do some stuff, help people with things in the community or fry some fish for my grandmother, things like that. He would always come home and take that nap first. The older I'd get, the more I think that it'd be neat to go home and take a nap every day at 4:00 or 4:30.

They had a big kitchen, and I remember many memories of my grandmother working in that kitchen making really, really good suppers. She made the best iced tea. Later, I'd have tea that was better sometimes, but I recently had a glass of tea, and it reminded me of my grandmother's tea. We had a lot of seafood meals in there. We were right by the water. My grandpa worked near the water, and he would come home with scallops or flounder or shrimp, and we'd fry them.

Sometimes, we'd fry in the backyard and sometimes we would fry them in the house. I remember many a really good meal right there around my grandmother's table with all the family around. It was a lot of fun doing that. My grandmother, especially, had fun because I loved to eat, and I have never outgrown that, as you can tell.

Out behind the house was a big garage. It wasn't where you parked your car. It's designed for that, but my grandfather used it for his shop, and it was a mess. You think my desk is a mess? You think I have clutter? My grandfather had every inch of that filled up! You could hardly walk! He just had a little tiny path through there. I remember one time when I was a little older, I started organizing that shop during the summer and cleaned it up. He walked in, and I think it was about the maddest he ever got at me because he said, "Son, now I can't find anything!" And I felt so bad. I thought I was going to make him happy, but here I made him sad because he couldn't find his stuff. Now I know what he meant.

Anyhow, one time, I went on a trip, and I told Bernadette, "Look, my desk is such a mess." I told her that story I just told you. And then I told her, "Forget all that and just go clean my office up. And if it looks important, just remember where you put it, and we'll start over."

So anyhow, I remember the next-door neighbors had a little boy named Richie. He was a year older than me, which seemed like a lot of difference, but I had a lot of fun hanging out with Richie. They had a really cool place. It seems like their place was a lot nicer than ours. They had a shop that was really neat and organized. On top of the shop, they had an apartment-like place, and that was really cool. Neighbors would stay there, and sometimes we'd go hang out there. We had fun running around together there.

I think the funnest part of going to my grandmother's house, though, was feeling all the love from my grandmother and my grandfather, my aunts and uncles, too, but especially my grandparents. They were very, very loving. All of them were loving to me, but my grandparents really took a lot of interest in me and did a lot for me, which is probably why I try to do that with my grandchildren, with each one of you.

Because, first of all, I love you very much. Second, it's just so much fun to watch you grow up, to see your lives change from one to two to three to four and to six, to 10, to 12, to 13 and beyond. And it's really exciting. It gives one courage. Sometimes when you're raising your own children, life is very busy, and you don't get to do all the things you want to do. Sometimes you're a little too impatient and a little too hard. I remember being that way with my children, with your parents.

But when you get older, you mellow out a little bit, and you're not as uptight. And you realize it wasn't that important to be uptight about this or that. I really could have backed off a little bit. You can't get a chance to do it over again with your own children, but it's fun and exciting to be more relaxed like that with your grandchildren.

I hope you have a lot of pleasant memories of Grandma and Grandpa's house or houses, since we have several. We have a lot of fun having you there, each one of you. It means a lot to me when you're at our house.

I hope when you read this story, maybe you're at one of Grandma's houses. Right now, she has a house in Pryor, Oklahoma, we have the house on the Powell farm, the pool house, and the apartment in Hartwell.

How much better can life be?

*Well, good night. I love you very much. Sweet dreams.*

*Grandpa*

## 14

*Cleaning the House*

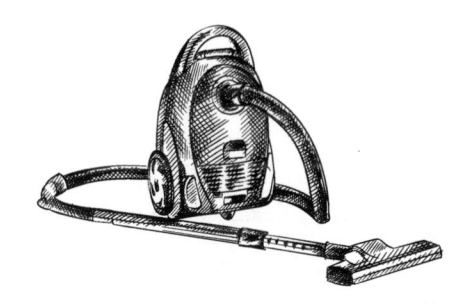

Do you help keep your house clean? What is your job? Our home was a three-bedroom, two-bathroom FHA 235 house. They called them FHA 235 because the Federal Housing Administration, which is what FHA stands for, would finance the house to a family for two percent down over thirty-five years. This meant you didn't have to have a lot of money for a down payment. The fact that they gave you thirty-five years to pay back the loan meant your payments were low enough for a young family or, in our case, a single mother with kids. Our house payments were eighty-one dollars a month!

You older kids might even be able to afford that now, but you have to remember money had a different value then. The minimum wage was $1.15 per hour versus $7.25 per hour now. A house like we had was $30,000. I think it would be $200,000 in today's market.

So to pay for our new house, my mother had to work very hard.

She was a waitress and bartender at a Holiday Inn. She went to work at 3:00 in the afternoon. We got off the school bus at 3:30 pm, so Mom was gone to work already. As I mentioned before, it was my responsibility to help look after my two sisters, Beth and Jerri Lynn.

After supper, we were to do our homework, watch TV, take our baths, and get to bed. I was supposed to make sure the house was kept clean. I took this job very seriously. I did the dishes. I'm not sure if we had a dishwasher or not. I vacuumed the floors every night. I'm not sure if it was messy or if I just thought it was messy. I do remember I wanted my mother to be happy with me and the job I did. This is a very good habit to have.

Are you happy with the job you do? Do you like to make your mom happy? I hope you say yes to this. If we learn to make our parents happy it will be easy to make our boss happy one day.

And remember, no matter what you do, we all have a boss. Of course, if you own your own business, the customer is your boss.

Also, if we learn this, it is easy to make our God happy by serving Him!

Well, I'm a last minute person. I always have been. I guess I always will be. I try not to be, but I still am. Are you a last minute person?

So, anyhow, we would sit around after we came in from playing outside, my sisters and I, and after we had supper, and after we watched Rampart 911, one of my favorite TV shows, and a few other shows. Finally, probably about 9:00, 9:30, I'd make them go to bed.

It was probably later if we really knew the truth of it all. And then, I would sit up and watch TV a little bit longer, relax after they were in bed. And then, about 10 o'clock, I'd tear in to cleaning the house up, wide open. I'd furiously go through and clean the kitchen, wash all the dishes, sweep the floor, go around vacuum the rooms, dust the tables.

I probably didn't do all this every night. I probably had some things I did different nights. But I would clean the house up, so that when my mother come home, everything was spic-and-span, nice and clean for Mom so that she would come home to a nice clean house. And obviously, she would come home and have no idea the chaos that had probably been there just a few hours before. It's probably good she didn't know what a mess it was!

But anyhow, that was my style of cleaning house. And I don't know if I've ever got a whole lot different than that. I know when grandma was traveling a lot, staying with Aunt Merita and different times with Jeremy and with Preston, and I'd be home alone.

A lot of times, I would want to have company on Sunday. And so on Saturday night I'd be up until late cleaning house, wide open, until late at night, getting it all done, last-minute. Then I could have company on Sunday.

So, I wonder, do you help your mom cleaning house? Do you do your share of the work? Do you like it when it's real clean? Or would you rather have a big mess?

I think most people like it clean. So, let's all do our part and help our moms clean house.

*Good night.*
*Love, Grandpa.*

*Don't be affected by peer pressure. Don't do what other people do just because they do. It can lead you down a path you don't really want to go.*

# 15

## *My First Money-Making Scheme*

My first money-making scheme is the name of this story. We all have one. A lot of times it's a lemonade stand or maybe making cookies, or maybe getting our dad or mom to pay for raking the leaves, mowing the grass or different things like that. And I think it's good we have that. I hope that everybody that listens to this story has had or will have one. If not, this may inspire you to. But I already know all of you that are old enough have probably already done this. So that's exciting.

So I think back to mine and I had those little ones, like I mentioned, about lemonade and cookies and that kind of thing. But I'm thinking about something a little bit more. What's your first little business that you launched? It seems like we all have one. I can tell you something about businesses I launched in school, but I don't think I'm going to get into that right now. I want to talk about good, hard, honest work.

So we lived in a new neighborhood. There were a lot of people.

## GRANDPA, TELL US A STORY

This is when I was about 11 years old. There were a lot of neighbors who had yards, what some people call postage stamp yards, but a little bit bigger than that. I mean, they're bigger than a postage stamp, but sometimes people call them that. Anyway, they weren't like our country yards that are two or three acres like Preston's yard, Jeremy's, or mine. They're more like maybe a quarter of an acre, probably. Probably not much more than that. Probably not a lot bigger than your houses are. A lot of people cut their own grass, but there were retired people and older people and busy young people, too. I would go door to door and say, "Hey, can I cut your yard for you?" They'd say, "How much?" I'd say, "$3." Then I took my lawnmower and cut the yard and they gave me $3.

Here's how I got the lawnmower. My mother went with me to the hardware store. This was in Augusta. I can still see the little hardware store. It was like a small, downtown kind of hardware store like they used to be, but this wasn't downtown. It was in a shopping plaza. It was a lot smaller store than the stores we have right now. That store was about like our Gibson store that we used to have that none of you will remember, but I would say it was around 4,000 square feet or 3,000 square feet. And our stores now are like 15,000 to 30,000 square feet. So it's a lot different.

Usually an old guy owned it. Maybe another old guy that helped him, maybe two brothers in business or something like that. Not a lot of extra people. You would go there and tell them what you needed and they'd help you find it. So my mother took me there and they had lawn mowers. I remember the lawnmowers were $29.97, and I thought, "That'll work. I can cut 10 yards to pay for my lawn mower." But I didn't have $29.97. And this is kind of the story of my life. Instead of waiting until I saved up the money, which my defense to that is, how can you save up the money if you can't make money? I needed the mower to make the $30 and I didn't have the mower.

So I was introduced to credit. Credit can be a friend and it can be an enemy. Depends on how you use it. You have to be very careful with it, but we won't get off on that tangent right now. We can talk about that later lest we digress a long ways. I have a lot of stories about that to tell you later.

So my mother took me there and she says, "My son would like to buy this lawn mower and he'll pay you over a couple months." And so the guy let me have the mower on credit in my mother's name. I was too little for him to trust me, I think, but he admired my energy. And I think I said that in another story. People will admire you if you're trying to do stuff. People respect that. We all do.

I admire that when I see it in each one of you, no matter how little. When I see little Liam trying to do things to help out, I know he's trying. He's doing the best he can do. And each one of you, I watch you help out. And it means a lot to me.

So that was my mower, $29.97. I was supposed to pay him like, I think $10 every two weeks. So I went home pumped. I was going to cut grass and make me a lot of money.

So I took my mower and I pushed it down the street, went knocking on doors. My first cold calling. Cold calling's a word that means when you go to try to sell something to somebody who didn't know they even wanted it. And it's not like you're delivering something. When you deliver it, that's fun. People tell you, "Hey, I need so and so." Or they call you up, "Will you come cut my grass?" "Shoot. yeah I'll do it."

"Cold calling is when you go knock on the door and you gather up all your courage and say, "Hello, Mrs. Smith, I saw your name on the mailbox and I'm anxious to make some extra money this summer. Can I cut your grass for $3?" And she says, "My grandson cuts it." Slams the door in your face. And you say, "Wow, you could at least be nice." Or they say "$3? That's a lot of money, son. When I was your age, I cut yards for a dollar."

Well, yeah, they probably did. That was a long time ago. And you negotiate. Maybe you settle for $2. You'll cut the yard because you're anxious to make a sale.

Or maybe they're real nice and they feel bad and say, "Sure, you can cut my yard for $3." And when you're done, they hand you a five dollar bill, and you feel like you really, really did something.

And so that was my first experience at cold calling, which is a good experience to have in life. It takes a lot of courage. It helps you overcome some barriers to dealing with people.

There I went, door-to-door. If I saw the grass was cut, I didn't go there. You know, no need in going there. If I saw Mr. Smith out with his mower, maybe a nice riding lawnmower, I knew there was no need to stop there. But I got jobs and I paid that mower off in those six weeks like I told the man. And I made some more money with it. I have no idea how much. I have no idea what I did with the money. I probably bought gifts for my family. I'd never been very good at saving money. If I'd let your grandmother handle all the money from the day we got married, I'd be sitting on a beach somewhere and wouldn't have had to work for the last 15 years, but I thought I was good at it.

One thing you have to figure out is what you're good at. I was not good at managing money. I was good at making money and could make lots of it, but I wasn't good at how I spent it. I wasn't careful enough. You need to learn to be careful with your money. I can't tell you what I did with all those $3, but I did save up a little money. I think I bought guns with it. That's probably what I spent my money on. I do have those guns today, so that's exciting.

I remember going back to that place and spending $59 for a shotgun that I saved up my money for. He didn't sell me that shotgun on credit. Because that wasn't really a necessity. That was just something I wanted. And that's the important thing. When you're buying things on credit, it needs to be something you can work with, you can make the money back and pay for it. We'll talk about that more later.

Right now, we're going to go to sleep. You're going to dream about your schemes and what you would do. I'd like to hear some of them.

*Goodnight, Grandpa*

# 16

*Pizza Hut!*

My first job was at Pizza Hut. I was probably 13 years old, and my mother worked at this Pizza Hut during the day. I think she may have worked three or four shifts a week. A shift at the Pizza Hut or a restaurant often is maybe four to six hours long. She was probably a waitress. That's what she did most of the time. So she probably had to go in about 9:30 or 10:00 in the morning to prepare for lunch and get the front ready. She was probably done with her shift around 2:00 or 3:00 in the afternoon.

And so it started out with me riding my bike three and a half or four miles to where she worked to see her and eat a pizza. I could get a discount on it, or she did, and so I could eat free probably, I don't know. But the owner was a really nice guy and he wanted to paint the place. He noticed that I didn't mind working, so he gave me a paintbrush. Bingo! I had my first job!

There I was, feeling important. Makenzie, right now you're 13. You can imagine how nice it feels to have a job making real money, your own money. I think he paid me a dollar and a half an hour or something. It was a lot of money. When I mowed a yard for three dollars, it took me all afternoon. Here I was making big money painting.

So I apparently did a good job and impressed the guy. It was summertime, and I took the trash out when I was waiting for paint to dry, or my mom to take me home, or something like that. Waiting on whatever you wait on when you're 13 years old and life and summertime hold a lot of time for you.

Anyhow, I would take the trash out, and sweep up around the kitchen. Again he noticed my eagerness to help out and paid me a little extra money for that. Soon I was working in the kitchen. He told my mother, "Bring that boy to work with you, I can use him."

That was my first experience bussing tables. I always enjoyed that, and I still do. When we had the Dutch House restaurant for years, I would go there to work many a night and bus tables. I like it. You feel like you're getting something done.

It's not for everybody. A lot of people don't like it, because it's a dirty job, or they think it's a lowly, demeaning job, which means that people think they're too good to do it, but it was fun to me. When I owned my own restaurant, it was absolutely important to me, because I could figure out what food people weren't eating, what they left on their plates, how much tips they left for the girls that were waitresses, or the guys that were waiters. I could learn a lot of things by seeing what was left on that table when they got done. And if somebody complained, I could say, "Well, that's a grumpy old guy, I'm not surprised." But there were a lot of things you can learn by bussing your own tables. Anyhow, I digressed again, but what's new!

So as it worked out, they taught me how to make pizzas at Pizza Hut. I remember doing that a lot. I remember taking that crust, laying it out on the pan and spreading it out, and putting the marinara sauce, the pizza sauce, and pepperonis and different meat on there. Sprinkling some hamburger on there, making anything

I wanted to, and putting some cheese on it, and putting it in the oven. The oven took 45 minutes to cook it. I think nowadays it takes about 15 minutes at The Bistro, because I hardly ever wait 45 minutes. Well, sometimes we do when they're real busy. So that was a lot of fun. I ate pizza every day, I just loved it. You can just imagine being 13 and having all the pizza you can eat.

Well, the summer ended, and I had to go back to school. That was the end of my job at Pizza Hut. I took home with me some of the ingredients so I could make my own pizzas, and I ate them for a while. But I remember not eating pizza, and not wanting to eat pizza for about two years after that, because I'd had enough pizza.

So anyhow, I'm wondering what your first job is going to be like. Some of you already have one. Makenzie, you help your dad in the auto sales, cleaning the office. And Kelby you've done lots of things, and Titus, you work at your dad's hardware store, and put up the order, and work with Grandpa sometimes. That's really cool.

And oh, my goodness, Dillan I've seen you putting light covers on receptacle covers in your dad's flip houses. And Hudson you're just a manager, dude. You like to figure things out and tell people what to do. Alexia's a real worker, too. She's got a good work ethic. Uncle Daniel says she'll work harder than anybody he has seen. He said, "She helped me stack firewood for a whole afternoon." And when she's at the store, you can give her jobs, then she'll go do them. She's a willing worker.

And Liam, I can already tell you're going to do lots of stuff. You're very willing to go help out. You always want to get your hands on things. I'm sure if Sawyer were here, he'd be just like that too. Probably even more so, because his mom was a hustler, too. She worked very, very hard.

Kate Eva, you're so little, I'm not sure yet. We'll see what you grow up and do.

*Good night all!*
*Grandpa*

*Credit can be a friend and it can be your enemy. Depends on how you use it. You have to be very careful with it.*

## 17

*Memory*

Your memory is an interesting thing. They say the average human has 60,000 thoughts per day. 85% or most of them are recurring, meaning they are memories you replay over and over. Like for me, I think of things I did in the first grade or even kindergarten, 54 years ago. A lot of these stories I can easily recall from my memory.

You each have your own memories. Makenzie at 11 years old has more than Alexia at five years old, but that's because she's been around six more years or 2,190 days more. There is a lot of memories made in 2190 days or in my case, 21,728 days!

I'm always impressed at how and what we remember. I think God made us in a way that we tend to remember the good more than the bad. For instance, if we took a trip to the water park and we had a lot of fun (like we did once) but had a really bad experience at a restaurant for lunch, we probably remember the water park and the restaurant memory fades away.

Now when something tragic or sad happens, I mean really sad like when Merita went to be with Jesus, we lock that in our memory too. We can usually remember exactly where we were when we heard the news of the tragedy. Now I don't want to get really sad here. I'm just talking about how memory works.

So, I wonder what are some of your favorite memories? Maybe you can tell the story tonight?

I think of memories way back to my life as a two-year-old in Germany with my mom and dad. My dad left my mom and us kids when I was only six years old. For the next 20 years the relationship between me and my Dad wasn't very good. It was actually very bad. We hardly spoke to each other and when we did it wasn't pleasant.

But after many years, 20 plus, we got together to try to reconcile and make up with each other. My dad brought a box of pictures and dropped it in front of me as I sat out in his backyard in North Carolina. I had told him I was hurt because he was never there with us when I was little.

Here in this box were pictures of us together in Germany and many other places and trips. As I looked at the pictures, I suddenly remembered us all being together.

You see I had only seen the pictures of my mom and me. She had taken those pictures and he had taken these other pictures when they split up. So, what I saw had "trained" my memory one way instead of how it really was.

I realized I had been wrong about my Dad all these years. Fortunately, God is good and we are able to forget the past and make new pleasant memories!

I hope you have only happy memories of me as your Grandpa!

*Love, Grandpa*

# 18

## *My First Watch*

I think I was six years old. Isn't that about when Kelby and Titus became obsessed about wanting a watch? Back then, there weren't as many choices of watches as there are today. It seemed like maybe six or seven styles to choose from. It's been a long time, so I can't recollect that, but this is what I remember.

It was a Timex® with a black leather band, and it was waterproof. Or maybe water-resistant? Kelby explained to Grandpa the difference once! Whichever it was, I was like most little boys with their first watch. I was very proud of it! I wore it everywhere. But it wasn't easy because I was really skinny. Yes, I know it's hard to believe now, but I was. My wrist was so small it was hard to get the watch tight on me, so the watch, being loose, often would catch on things.

We went on a vacation to visit my great-grandparents in Oklahoma and then to Loveland, Colorado, to see my grandparents on the Bullock side. I loved to swing on the swing set in Grandma's backyard. Looking back, she must have put it up for me as I was the first grandchild. She was a very sweet Grandma like yours is!

Well, as I was saying, one day, the watchband caught on the swing chain as I jumped off, and it broke the band. The watch went flying in several pieces, and I was very sad. I'm sure I cried as that's what we do when we're sad. It's okay to cry. My dad told me that years later when I was crying because he and my Mom didn't live together and I missed him a lot. I never forgot it.

And I never forgot that watch. Dad tried to fix it, but that was hopeless. I decided not to get another one, and I have never worn a watch again. I doubt I ever will. I do not like anything that goes on my wrist or, for that matter, around my neck.

When I was ten, I wanted to be a hippie like my Uncle Charlie Bullock. I got a big gold medallion neck chain for Christmas, and I wore that for a while, but that's the only thing I ever put around my neck. I don't let Jenny Kay put the hair-cutting apron tight around my neck even! She always laughs at me. That's okay.

Later on, I noticed my Grandpa Burt had a pocket watch, and I liked that. I started carrying one of those when I was 15 or so. Grandma bought me a couple of nice ones over the years. But eventually, I got away from carrying that too. I can usually tell you the time within ten minutes anyhow as I think I subconsciously measure time all day long. Of course, nowadays, we have the time right on our cell phones and computers and in our vehicles.

Do you wear a watch? What kind is it? Who gave it to you? Is it just a watch, or is it special to you?

Looks like it's bedtime now!

*Goodnight!*
*Grandpa*

# 19

## *Memories of My Grandfather Burt*

So, this would be your great, great grandfather! Now that sounds like a long time ago, and I guess it is kind of, but these memories are still very fresh on my mind. I called him Granddad. His name was James Alexander Aloysius Burt.

He was a tall man with a big belly, yes kind of like mine! You can giggle now. He was mostly bald as long as I can remember. He smoked a pipe with always the same tobacco. I can still remember the smell. Back then, a lot of people smoked cigarettes, some cigars, but not very many used a pipe.

I don't think smoking is good for anyone at all. I can only imagine how harmful it is to breathe all that smoke directly in your lungs. So please, please do not ever smoke. I try not to even breathe in second hand smoke from people. When I was growing up, there was smoking everywhere, restaurants, stores, and nearly everywhere you went.

So, as I rode in my granddad's work van, he had his pipe going, and I would roll down my window to let the smoke out. Unfortunately, that just pulled it past me all the more. But that's just a little memory of Granddad.

He worked for the railroad. I remember hearing him getting up at 4:30 in the morning and getting ready for work. He came home around 3:30 in the afternoon. The first thing he did was to plunk down in his recliner and kick back. In just a minute or less he was snoring away. He'd nap for about an hour then get up for supper.

Many times, we'd eat seafood since we lived only ten minutes from the ocean. He had lots of friends who owned fishing boats. They'd say, "Burt, you need some scallops?" He'd say, "Don't know that I need 'em, but I'll take 'em."

No, not really. He was a man of few words, so what he'd say is, "Yup," or maybe he'd just wink at his friend. Soon we were lugging bags or boxes of fresh scallops or flounder out to his old white van.

So after he napped, we might head out back of the house to clean some flounder fish for supper. I'd watch close as Granddad cut the heads off the fish and filleted our supper. Do you know how to clean a fish?

My grandmother would cook whatever we prepared for her, and I ate many a delicious meal around that table. Once supper was done, we'd jump in the van and head off to fix something for someone, or he would dress up and go to AA meetings but more on that later! See, sometimes I don't digress!

*More another night!*
*Grandpa*

# 20

## *Granddad Burt's Van*

The old white van was quite a van. Nothing – I mean nothing – fancy. Plain, bare bones work van. No AC. Never ever do I remember him washing it, probably why I never think of washing my vehicles! The back of the van was full of junk. Well, he wouldn't call it junk. It was all the things he needed to fix washing machines or dryers or fridges or air conditioners or plumbing or electrical problems. Granddad could fix about anything! He had no formal training or education. He just learned it along the way, a lot like your dads did, but Granddad could do a lot more than them. Or me for that matter!

He always seemed to know where to find whatever he needed in the messy pile of parts. He'd say, "Boy, go get my tool bag." (He always called me Boy!) I learned the names of each kind of tool from him. When I'd get the wrong one, he'd scold me gently then teach me the right name for the tool. I soon learned that a tool could have more than one name. Like a conduit bender isn't simply a conduit bender; it can also be referred to as a hickey. "Boy, get my ½ inch hickey."

Off I'd go to the van plundering around looking for whatever a hickey is! Growing impatient, he'd come looking for me and grab the conduit bender. I'd ask why he didn't ask for the conduit bender if that's what he wanted. He'd just laugh his little chuckle. I just realized I deal with this every day as people come in the hardware store using their own jargon and language to describe something in the most confusing way possible!

The things I learned on those repair calls with my Granddad have helped me immensely throughout my life. I once put in my own AC unit in my first mobile home after Grandma and I were married. I wired up a couple houses completely by myself and lots of other smaller jobs. It's that knowledge that helps me sell lighting jobs today.

But back to the van. Oops, I digressed. Again! One summer I decided to help my Granddad out. While he was at work, I drug everything out of the van and then organized it and put it all back in. I was so proud of how neat it now was. I couldn't wait for him to come home to see my surprise! He was surprised alright! But not so happy.

Again, he wasn't a man of a lot of words, but I could tell he was close to being mad. In my young mind I couldn't understand why he wouldn't be delighted. Looking back now, I realize he had memorized where everything was, and I had messed with his system. I learned to accept his mess and decided that one day if I ever had my own work van, I would be more organized.

Today I do have a couple of vans, and they are not as organized as I'd like, but I do tell Bernadeth when I go out of town, "Clean the van up!" and I am happy.

*Goodnight! Grandpa*

## 21

*Mayor Burt*

Most of their lives, my grandparents Burt lived at 37 Westover Street in Hampton, Virginia. I shall always remember that address. Probably because it was one of the first addresses I learned. I remember carefully writing it on envelopes for letters and cards I'd lovingly send them.

Now I get letters and cards from you guys and gals. Oh, how exciting it is too! Grandma and I read those letters over and over and put them on the fridge to remind us of the love from afar.

After my granddad retired, they would come to Georgia to visit us. These were always exciting times. One summer, I think it was 1977, and I was 17. We moved to a very large farm in Mitchell, Georgia. My granddad loved chatting with the old guys at the Haywood's Convenience store in Mitchell.

The locals soon found out my granddad's talents, and he was in high demand fixing all their plumbing, electrical and HVAC needs. HVAC is an abbreviation for heating, ventilation, and air conditioning.

Granddad bought a small mobile home and set it up at the corner of our yard. Granddad would have me bring home supplies from Avera Hardware where I worked so we could do jobs in the evenings and weekends. Those are great memories of us working together. Do we do enough stuff together?

Later we moved off the farm and Granddad moved his mobile home into a lot in town. The city of Mitchell convinced Granddad he could watch over the city water system. Looking back, I thought he was an old man. I think he was 57, younger than I am as I pen these words by two years.

Somewhere along the way he served on the city council and then was elected mayor of Mitchell. I'm not sure how long he held this title and I wonder if Mitchell even has a mayor today? Back then the population was probably around 200!

Would you want to be mayor?

My first boss at Avera Hardware said, "Stay out of politics. You think everyone likes you, but then when you don't get enough votes you feel all sad!"

Maybe we'll settle for mayor of our bedroom!

*Good night!*
*Grandpa*

## 22

*My First Trip to the Farm*

When I was 14, my mother met Andy Isaac. They started dating, and I thought Andy was really neat. He was younger than my mother by nine years. That made him only eleven years older than me, so he was kind of like a big brother and a dad to me. Andy's parents were Mennonites and lived in Davisboro, Georgia, about an hour away from Augusta.

I always loved the woods and wide-open spaces. So when Andy offered to take me to his parent's dairy farm to go hunting, I was very excited. I loved animals. I had eight dogs, two cats, a turtle, some fish, and a parakeet. I dreamed of lots more!

That ride to the farm seemed like it took four hours, not one. I stared out the window while "riding shotgun" the whole way. I was sure I'd see deer and who knows what kind of wildlife everywhere. Well, it wasn't quite like that. As a matter of fact, I didn't see any animals until we got to the farm. What I did see was lots of wide-open spaces. It was awesome. I remember thinking that one place looked really nice, and I dreamed of owning it. Twenty years later, I bought that piece of land. Again, I digress.

Not only had I never seen a cow up close, but I also had no idea what Mennonites were and why the ladies had those black things on their heads, and the men all looked like mountain men or Father Time with their beards. I didn't study that much, though, as the cows had my attention.

It seemed like there were hundreds of them. In reality, it was only 45 grown cows and 25 to 30 calves. But I was too busy enjoying it all to stop and count the cows! I was running here and there, checking out everything as fast as I could. It was all so exciting to me, and I loved it. I didn't want to go home at the end of the day.

At lunch, it seemed like there were 50 people at the table, likely it was twelve to fifteen, something we are used to now, but for this city kid, it was a big deal. I got to ride on the tractor for the first time, which was way cooler than pretending at the construction site!

Even now, looking back 47 years, that day seemed to last for a week. I was hooked. I knew I wanted to live in the country. And I live on a farm now nearly 50 years later. I used to live 20 feet from my neighbors, now I am two miles from my nearest neighbor, and I like that.

Do you like where you live? I think no matter where you live, you need to be happy. I was happy in Augusta, and I am happy now. Happy is a good way to be!

*Good night and happy dreams!*
*Love, Grandpa*

# 23

## *Milking Cows*

We moved to the farm in Davisboro when I was 14 years old, probably a month before my 15th birthday. My new grandparents, my stepdad's parents, were Paul and Mary Isaac. We called them Papa and Mama Isaac. They had a dairy farm with about 40 cows. It was a family operation. I had never been around cows in my life. I had never milked a cow. It was all new.

As I've told you before, I loved animals. Animals were fun to me. I had eight dogs. I had two or three cats. I had a turtle, fish, and a parakeet. My mother let me have just about any kind of animal I'd bring home. I had a chicken. I loved animals.

But I thought cows were the greatest thing that ever happened to me. I fell so much in love with milking cows that I decided I wanted to spend the rest of my life doing that. I couldn't wait to get out of school so I could milk all the time and eventually have my own dairy farm. I spent a lot ... well, I'll get into those stories another time, but I spent probably ten years of my life, maybe more, trying to become a dairy farmer before I finally gave up on that. It's a hard way to make a living, but if you want to do it, go for it. There's no way to know until you try. One thing about dairy farming: after you do it, everything else in life is easy.

But back to my story here, I digressed again. What's new? They had these 40 cows that had to be milked, and you have to milk the cows twice a day, morning and evening. And this is not an eight to five job I'm talking about, or a nine to five. You ideally ought to milk the cows about 4:30 or 5:00 in the morning, before it gets too hot, and then 12 hours later, about 4:30 in the afternoon. Because if you did it at eight in the morning, you'd have to do it at eight in the evening, and it'd ruin all your evenings. So if you want to be done by about 6:30 or 7:00 in the evening, and it takes about two and a half hours to milk, that means you need to start at 4:00 in the evening. So that means you need to start about 4:00 in the morning.

You can kind of fudge a little bit. 4:30 was our starting time in the morning and 4:00 in the afternoon. So my alarm would go off at 4:00 and out of the bed I'd get. If it was cold, you bundled up. You put on enough clothes so you wouldn't be cold and you put your chore boots on.

Nowadays, there's all kinds of four-wheelers and side-by-sides and things like that, but we didn't have any of that back then. What we did was, I went out the back door of my house and took off walking. It was about a quarter-mile to the barn, which isn't that bad of a walk, but I had to get the cows up as I walked down there. The trouble was the gate. It was shut down at the bottom end. So I'd walk down the field, getting the cows up. And that was kind of a zig-zagging around saying, "Whoa Bossy, whoa Bossy, get up, girls. Let's go." And you'd talk to them a little bit, stir them up. And there would always be some contrary one, but you tried to get them all to go the same way. You got 40 cows, and they're all over the field. Later on in my life, I'd milk 150, and I'd do the same thing. But at this point, I was finding 40 cows, waking them all up. I'd take a flashlight. It's dark at 4:30 in the morning.

How many of you get up at 4:30 in the morning? I wonder if any of you ever have to. Maybe if you're going on a trip or something, but I think most of the time, you all leave a little later than that. Anyhow, then I'd get them down toward the barn. I'd have to run around ahead of them and open the gate to where they need to go into milk. Then I would walk back around behind them again and push them on up there.

I know Titus right now would be thinking, "I'd have a horse, and I'd do that." Kelby would probably say the same thing. Or he'd say, "I'd get a motorcycle, and I'd do it." Well, I had all those dreams too, just like you boys do, but I didn't have a horse. I didn't have the money for one. I didn't have a motorcycle dream because I'm not very good with anything with only two wheels, but I sure dreamt about having a four-wheeler a lot. Dillan would say, "That's what I'd do." I believe it. I'm sure Hudson would too. When Liam gets older, that's probably what he'll think, but Grandpa didn't have none of that, so we walked. I walked. Ain't no we to it. It was just me.

I woke them cows up, got them up to the barn, and shut the gate on them. Then you have to go turn the lights on, hook all the hoses up, get everything going, and start the pumps. Then you can milk the cows. We had what was called a single-three barn. It had three cows on one side. Each cow stood in their individual stall and you stood in the "pit," which was about three feet lower. This kept you from having to lean over.

So you'd open the gate in the stall that holds the cow, and you'd go out and get a cow and drive her up in the milking parlor. Then you shut the gate on her, spray her off, and wash off her tits where the milkers go on her udders. You clean all that up because there'd be mud on them, and you don't want mud in your milk. You'd make chocolate milk. That's not really good. There ain't no such thing as a cow giving chocolate milk, by the way. They give white milk.

So, anyhow, you want to make sure it's clean, so there's not a lot of junk in your milk. Then you hook the milking machine up to the cow, which sucks the milk out of them. And it goes in a pipeline, and the pipeline carries the milk into a big tank. When the milk comes out of the cow, it's about probably 78 degrees. It's fairly warm, but it won't last long like that. You have to put it in a big tank with a cooling thing in it, and it cools it down to about 38 degrees.

And so you milked all the cows. A cow will give about nine gallons of milk nowadays. Back then, they gave about, I don't know, they gave probably about five gallons of milk. Through better genetics and feeding cows better, they give a lot more milk nowadays.

And after you get all the milk out of the cow, you'd take the milking machine off, open the gate and let them go. So you start with one, and then you get that one going, you put your second cow in, get her going. Put the third cow in, get her going. And by that time, your first cow was probably done. And then you'd let that one go and bring another one in. And you just kept going like that back and forth. It took a little time.

Later on we had a bigger barn that would milk more cows. You could do it a lot faster. In that barn, we fed them. So we'd put some feed up in front of them. So you had to fill up the feeders, and they'd get a chance to eat while they're standing there. And that would help them stand still so they'd let you milk them without kicking you.

Sometimes they weren't too used to it, and they'd kick you, and boy did it hurt. It'd make you just so mad, and you might say something you shouldn't. Do you ever get that mad, so mad that you say something you shouldn't? It sure made me that way a lot of times.

And then it'd be so cold in the winter in that barn. Oh, it was cold. The wind blew right through there. I had two heaters going in there, one burning wood and one burning kerosene, and I'd run them wide open. And you could stand between those heaters and about freeze to death. It was tough. You can't have a coat on because you got to be washing the cows with your hands, so your arms are exposed from your elbows down. And you're in water. You use a lot of water. So it's something you get very cold when you're doing. And I did that for about two years.

Now, I told you about cutting grass, making three dollars a yard. I got paid $20 a week to milk cows. Now that might sound like a lot of money to you, but I tell you what, I got up every morning and went down and milked those cows. I came home after school, and I milked those cows. I did this seven days a week. Sometimes I would get one day off if someone could fill in for me because cows have to be milked seven days a week. It was a lot of work for $20. I could have cut a lot of yards in that time. I think I could've probably made about three times that much money cutting yards in a week.

Of course, I couldn't get up and cut a yard before I went to school when I lived in the city. And never mind about the money because I was just happy to be doing it. Sometimes if you like something well enough, it doesn't have to make so much money. Believe that or not, Kelby.

Anyhow, when you do a job, you want to do a job you like, not a job that just makes a lot of money. They say if you do what you like, you never go to work a day in your life. You just go do what you want to do, and that's so true.

*Okay, sweet dreams. We all got to get up at 4:30 and milk in the morning.*

*Grandpa*

*One thing about dairy farming: after you do it, everything else in life is easy.*

# 24

## *The Hyatt Place*

When I was 17 years old, we moved off the farm in Davisboro. It was one of the most heartbreaking moves I'd ever made. I just loved that farm. I loved working on the farm with the dairy and all the cattle, getting up and milking cows in the morning, and feeding calves. All the things were fun and exciting to me.

I imagined me and my stepdad, Andy Isaac, working there for the rest of our lives. It seemed like one of the funnest things that happened to me. That was because it was, not because it seemed like it. It was a lot of fun. I know a lot of people would think it'd be a lot of work, but for me, it was pure fun. It wasn't all easy, but it was fun.

But it didn't work for Andy to buy the farm from his dad, Papa Isaac, as we called him. That would be my Grandpa Isaac. Gerald Giesbrecht was able to buy the farm, so we had to move.

We first moved to Stapleton. I talked about that in another

story. If I didn't, I will. All at once, I found this ad in the local newspaper about somebody wanting someone to live on their place and look after it for very cheap rent. This person's name was Bill Hyatt. I believe that's his name. It's been a long, long time.

He had this place in Mitchell. Mitchell is on the other side of Gibson, which is on the other side of our store in Wrens. It's about 25 miles from the store in Wrens. It's out in the boonies, as I say. The nearest store was Haywood's store, which was kind of like a convenience store right in the town of Mitchell.

After that, you could go to Gibson, which wasn't much bigger. Gibson had Chalker and Sons Hardware, which many, many years later, we bought. It was our first hardware store.

It also had a little hamburger joint, and it had a little local grocery store, Kitchen's Grocery.

Anyhow, I found this place, this ad in the paper. I was so excited. Of course, Andy didn't believe in my ideas right away, so he was very hesitant to look at it, but I arranged an appointment for us to go look at it on one Saturday.

We went up there, and it was 923 acres. It had a house on it, a fairly new brick home about three or four years old. The house had hardly been lived in, a very nice house. Best as I remember, it was a three or four-bedroom house. It looked out over a pasture behind it.

In that pasture right out back, just the perfect distance, was a nice horse barn. There were even a couple of Shetland ponies out there, which was close enough to a horse for me at that age. There might've even been another horse. I can't remember, but I think it was just those Shetlands.

Past that was all these acres you could hunt on. Then at the very back of the place was the Ogeechee River, one of the largest rivers around here. Probably the largest one would be the Savannah River up near Augusta. The Ogeechee was a nice river for hunting on, fishing in, just everything a 17-year-old boy could dream of, or a

12-year-old boy or 10-year-old boy or 15-year-old boy or 50-year-old boy or a 70-year-old boy. It was a very, very nice place.

On that river, after a long, winding trail way back to it, there was a cabin built on the bluff. A bluff is kind of like a cliff up over a river or over anything, for that matter. There was this cabin. It was a perfect little cabin. Best as I remember, it was like a one-bedroom cabin with a little kitchen in it. It had a screened-in porch on the back. It sat about, I'm guessing, about 25 feet up over the river on this bluff, like I said, and looked down on the river. It was just awesome. I could've just lived there.

Of course, it was a long way back there, probably a half mile ride back through the woods. Back then, it seemed like forever. It was a long ride, but nowadays, if I had it to do over again, I would just live there. As it was, it was a great place to escape to and have a cookout.

Looking back, we didn't use it near enough. Although your grandmother and I used it a little bit in our courting days. We would go back there and sit there on that porch looking down at the river, and cuddle with each other. I remember those memories very, very fondly. Since this is a children's bedtime story, maybe I'll stop right there on those memories. That could be in another storybook.

Anyhow, we went and looked at this place, and he agreed to let us rent this place, if I remember right, for $150 or $175 a month. He really wanted a caretaker for the place and just a little bit of income off of it. It was an awesome deal.

Nowadays, people would probably pay maybe $500 a month just for the hunting rights on that piece of land. The hunting was awesome. The land stretched down the road for probably a mile and a half. It was on each side of the highway at one point. I did some of the finest, best, funnest deer hunting in my life on that 923 acres. I killed a lot of deer there.

We had friends come and hunt there. One of my friends killed the biggest buck I've ever seen around here almost, probably one of the biggest ones, on that piece of land.

It's funny. He wasn't somebody everybody liked very much. He wasn't a real close friend of mine. We let him hunt in this stand because he wanted to go really bad, and there'd already been about six bucks killed from it, so we figured all those bucks were gone, and maybe he'd kill a small one or a doe. Well, he kills the biggest one that's ever been killed on the place there. That was exciting, too.

I remember one morning Andy had two bucks come up underneath his stand and start fighting. I think he killed them both. I can't remember for sure.

I would spend hours walking that land, hunting. I remember doing my first turkey hunting in my life there and had a turkey answer me and saw my very first turkey.

I shot a hoot owl there once. You really shouldn't shoot hoot owls, but he flew up in front of me and landed on a limb, and I shot him with my 30-30. It was exciting.

I bow hunted on that place with my very first bow, and missed a great big buck there. I had a lot of fun.

Later on, Andy and I got some hogs. We had some sows. That's a big female hog. They would have pigs.

Then we'd sell the pigs. They're called feeder pigs. They get about 40 or 50 pounds when you sell them, sometimes 30 pounds if the market was right, and so I'd sit up at night with hogs while they had pigs. That's a whole 'nother story, too.

That place was one of the funnest and coolest places. Every time I drive by it now, I think what a cool place.

What's the funnest place you ever lived on, and what made it fun to you?

I lived in a lot of different places in my life. I don't even know the count of it by now. I would guess I probably lived in 20 different places, maybe more, maybe 25. A lot of them have been fun in a lot of different ways.

Right now, as I write this, I live on the Powell Farm, as we call it, which is where your grandmother grew up. It was where your great-grandfather, Pop, grew up as a kid. I think even your great-great-grandfather grew up there. So a lot of Powells lived on that place.

I like it because it's real quiet. When I first moved back there, I wasn't real enthused, but Grandma wanted to move back there because, well, that's a whole 'nother story, like I say, and I'll tell you that later.

Anyhow, after I got to living there, I really, really liked it. I still like it.

The Bible has a verse that says be content wherever you are. That's not exactly how it is, but that's what it means. That's really important, to be happy and content wherever you are.

Right now, hopefully, you're in bed, ready to go to sleep. So be content and be happy and be thankful.

*Good night.*
*Love, Grandpa*

*One thing you have to figure out is what you're good at. I was not good at managing money. I was good at making money and could make lots of it, but I wasn't good at how I spent it. I wasn't careful enough. You need to learn to be careful with your money.*

# 25

## *Peer Pressure*

I started telling this story a little bit in another story, so I'll go on from there. On the Hyatt place is where I first got in the hog business. I never had any hogs before, never knew much about them. I don't know what propelled us to get into them, but thinking back, I remember a lot of people right around Mitchell were getting into it, so it's probably like a lot of other things, probably peer pressure.

Do you know what peer pressure is? Peer pressure is when you do things because other people around you are doing them. That's not always a good idea. Sometimes, it can be.

There's a saying, "When you're in Rome, do like Romans do." That's kind of true. If you live in a certain place and the custom is to take your shoes off when you go in the house, you should probably do that. That's a good custom for that area. You should go with it. If you're living in a foreign country and they do things a certain way, you should probably do that.

When it comes to peer pressure, it's just slightly different. That's not always the best thing to do. It can be. It can be a good thing to do like your peers are doing. You know what peers are? That's like your friends or people around you. They might not even be your friends. They might just be a similar group of people like you are. They might be like the people in the community, the people in Wrens or the people in Pryor, Oklahoma or the people in Hartwell, Georgia or the people who live in Center, Colorado. It's kind of nice to be part of a group.

It's called peer pressure because people feel pressured to do what people around them are doing. I remember when I went to school, sometimes the other kids would all slip off around the corner of the playground and smoke. There was a lot of pressure to smoke like they did. I didn't want to smoke. I didn't think that was a good thing. I couldn't imagine how that was good for your body to pull that smoke in your body. It just did not look healthy to me. I never did like it.

My parents smoked when I was little. I did not like that. I did not like the smell of smoke. It just did not excite me at all. There was a lot of pressure. Because to be cool, everybody was smoking.

"Cool." You know, sometimes people do dumb things that they think are cool. That's not always cool. Sometimes, it's cool to be different. Don't ever be scared of that.

Somehow or another I dodged all that. I'm trying to think. It seems like one time, I actually put a cigarette to my mouth and tried it. I remember hacking and coughing and thinking that was not cool. That was not fun. I don't see how anybody liked that. From then on, I never, ever tried it.

I'll actually back up and tell you the reason I don't like cigarettes or beer. When I was a little kid, my real dad, Jerry Bullock, was a military man. He was in the Army. When you join the Army, you kind of work your way up through the ranks. You start out as just a private, I think they call it, which is basically the lowest person on the totem pole. I was going to say lowest man, but nowadays, there's men and women in the Army. That's okay, too.

Anyhow, my dad, he was the lowest man on the totem pole. He was just getting started. To climb the ranks, you do your job well, like you do with any job, and you get a promotion, a higher rank and, eventually, another one. Then you can make officer.

You think about like in our hardware stores, a lot of times, people start out as a cashier. Years ago, we used to just have people who swept the floor and put stuff together. Nowadays, it's kind of all a little bit more targeted and defined and people do certain jobs. When I started out, I swept the floor and I put bikes together. Eventually, I could wait on people. Eventually, I could run the cash register. Later, I became a manager, so I worked up through the ranks. That's the way the Army works.

My dad, he wanted to work up the ranks, as all of us are aggressive people. As he made officer, he'd have different people over to his house for social events, kind of a get-to-know-the-bigwigs so that they'll put in a good word for you when they see Jerry Bullock's promotion come up.

"Oh, yeah, I was with him and his wife at their house," they might say. "He grilled us steaks. We had a great time. He's a great guy. I was really impressed with him. Want to make sure he gets that promotion."

A lot of times, other people decide what is good for you when you're working in a company and operation like that.

Anyhow, my dad and mom would have these nice, big parties at their house. A lot of times, I remember getting tucked into bed at about 7:00. As I was sleeping, I could also hear the laughing and drinking and music going on downstairs. They would drink beer and wine and eat, stuff like that.

Nowadays, you kids grow up and you're involved in whatever we do. Of course, we don't do all that partying like that with drinking alcohol and beer and all, but we have friends over. Sometimes, we call it get togethers or social evenings. It's all kind of the same thing. Anyhow, you're often involved in it. That's nice.

I know your parents, my kids, they were always involved in what we did. We didn't do things without them. We always did things with them. That was nice. We have a lot of good memories from that.

Anyhow, they would have these parties. They'd probably last until about midnight and everybody would go home. Well, I get up in the morning, having gone to bed at 7:00. I'd probably get up about 5:00 in the morning, 5:00 or 6:00. Of course, my parents, they'd be sound asleep.

You know how your parents are when you wake up sometimes. You get up in the morning and they say, "Be quiet. We're still sleeping." I know especially Dillan, he always gets up early in the morning. Hudson gets up pretty early, too. Titus, he gets up early. Most of the rest of y'all kind of sleep in.

I got up and I went downstairs. There were cans of beer sitting around where everybody drank most of them. There'd be just a little bit left in the bottom of the can. As a little kid, I thought that was cool. I'd drink me a beer, at least the last little bit of one.

Don't you try this. This isn't good. This is what I did. I grabbed those beer cans, tilted them up, and got that last, little swig out of there. As a kid, it tasted kind of good to me.

Well, a lot of people would use those cans for an ashtray. They'd be smoking and they'd put their ashes out in it. They might not have ashtrays sitting around.

Fortunately, you don't know much about smoking, but when you smoke the cigarette makes ashes and they have to go somewhere. They'll burn the furniture and they'll burn the carpet because they're hot when they fall off and so you need an ashtray and to put them out on.

Of course, now hardly anybody ever smokes inside. That's all changed in our world, but back then, people did. They smoked everywhere. In their cars. In their houses. We just all grew up around smoke. You smoked or else you breathed it in from other people. I'm so thankful it's not that way anymore, smoking in stores and restaurants and things like that. Now, it's not that way, and that's good.

Anyhow, some people used their cans for an ashtray. A lot of times, you could see the ashes on them. Well, I picked up a can and it had a little bit more beer in it. I thought, "Wow, I got me a good one here." Well, I turned it back and drank it.

And somebody had used it for an ashtray. Here was this can of half beer and half ashes. Now, that is really, really nasty. I turned that can back and got it in my mouth and started drinking. Before I could stop, I was swallowing all that junk and oh, it was awful. I could hardly hack it. I quickly went and got something to wash it down and clear my mouth out with. And I never ever wanted anything to do with a beer or a cigarette ever again.

Right now, as I tell you this story 56 years later or 57, I don't know, it's been a long time, about 56 years ago, it still makes me sick to think about it.

Not long ago, I was at a restaurant by myself, a nice seafood place. The waiter comes to me. He said, "You look like a Yuengling kind of fellow."

I thought, "A Yuengling? What in the world do I look like?"

Well, it's a kind of beer, I realized, and I didn't have to show my ignorance too much. He was suggesting that I might want a beer to go with my meal.

I said, "Actually, no, thank you. I'll take water."

Now lately, I've started drinking sweet tea again. For years, I drank a lot of sweet tea. Then I quit and drank only water for about five years. I've been drinking a little tea again. It kind of helps me focus a little bit.

Which brings me to the point of why people drink beer and why they do different things, different drugs even, in life. It's because they think they get certain benefits from them.

Even like tea, it has caffeine in it. Caffeine is kind of like a drug. It can help you in some ways. In some ways, it doesn't help you. It keeps you awake. It's a stimulant. It also can help you focus because, again, you're stimulated, but that can all be negative after a while, too.

When I quit drinking caffeine six years ago, I felt like I was 10 years younger right away, so it's probably like a lot of other things. A little bit of it would be okay, but if you do too much of it, it's probably not good for you.

A lot of people drink coffee in the morning because it has caffeine and wakes them up. I don't need anything to wake me up. Like Makenzie, it probably helps her wake up in the morning. She's kind of a sleepy-eyed person in the morning. She wakes up slow and that's okay. Some people are that way.

Aunt Merita was that way. I don't remember her drinking coffee, but I know when she woke up, it took her a little bit to get going before she was just ready to tackle the world.

I've never been like that. I wake up. I'm ready to go. It's okay either way. You can be both ways. It's no problem. Everybody's different.

Well, this story got long, so it will have to be continued.

The moral of this story is don't be affected by peer pressure. Don't do what other people do just because they do. It can lead you down a path you don't really want to go.

You can have all the ideas you want with your life and all the dreams. If you follow somebody else's, you're not going to get where you want to go.

It's like going down a road. If you know how to go down the road to get from Hartwell to Wrens or from Pryor to Tulsa, you know the way, and somebody else says, "Hey, go this way. It'll work, too."

It might. It might work. It also might take you on the wrong path. It might be a long way to get there. You might get lost. You might end up where you don't want to be, so it's best to have your own direction and go where you want to go without somebody else influencing you.

Now, if they want to influence you to the good, that's a good thing. There's nothing wrong with that. Sometimes, it's positive peer pressure, where you have like your friends in youth group or friends in your church or friends in school that are good people and doing the right thing.

Even then, you want to make sure and have your own direction. That's really important.

*I'm going to say good night at that. We'll keep going in another story.*

*Grandpa*

*I wanted my mother to be happy with me and the job I did. This is a very good habit to have. Are you happy with the job you do? Do you like to make your mom happy? I hope you say yes to this. If we learn to make our parents happy it will be easy to make our boss happy one day... Also, if we learn this, it is easy to make our God happy by serving Him!*

# 26

## *The Bear Cat*

Well, our last story was on peer pressure. It was supposed to be about hogs. I got off topic there, so I'll try to get a little more on topic here and keep going. I had never had any experience with hogs. I got onto peer pressure because I think that's what influenced us to do it.

Andy heard about people having hogs and making a lot of money with them. He thought it'd be a good thing. We could start off small. We could buy about 10 sows. You could buy them for, I want to say, 50 bucks, so for $500, we were in the hog business.

Well, we had to grow them up. They needed to get a little bit bigger. Before they can have pigs, they need to be about 225 pounds, so we had to feed them. That didn't seem so bad. We could buy a little feed here and there.

I remember I used to take the pickup to get the feed. The Hyatt farm came with a pickup, a blue Chevrolet pickup. It had a nice, long bed. The best that I remember, it was a stick shift. It was actually on the column, three on the column, they called it. You would shift gears with the clutch. I won't get off on a sidetrack with that right now.

Anyhow, I would take that pickup to work with me. Then I would go to Cliff Martin Milling Company on my lunch break. It was a feed place in Wrens. The Martins had a great, big feed mill, so that's a whole 'nother story. I could talk about it. I probably should, but we'll go back to that another day.

Anyhow, it's funny how one story leads to another. That's the way life is. Life is all about stories. You're writing the story with your life. You may think these are cool Grandpa's stories. I hope they are, but you each one have your own cool stories, too. There's cool stories about Makenzie and Titus and Kelby and Alexia and Dillan and Hudson and Liam and Amelia and Kate and Robbin. They're all cool stories. There's cool stories your moms and dads have to tell you. You just got to make them tell them to you.

Anyhow, I digressed again. Getting back on the story, I would take that pickup to town when I went to work. I'd go to Cliff Martin's Milling Company. They would put grain on the back of it. I'd buy some barley or oats or corn, take it home with me, and I'd grind it up.

I used a feed grinder that we hooked to a tractor. You'd shovel that corn into there, and it'd grind it up. That way, the hogs can get more value from it when they ate it. You mix in some meal with it and some protein like soybean meal or soybeans, and you'd have a nice feed that would make the hogs grow good. They could've just ate the corn, but corn has like 9% protein in it. You mix that corn together with some soybean meal that has 40% protein, and you could end up with about a 14% feed. The hogs would grow better on that.

Now, that feed grinder we used to grind that feed, that's a whole story in itself. I'm going to stop and tell that story in a little bit before I forget it.

When we lived in Davisboro and had the dairy farm, we used a feed grinder. It was a Bear Cat feed grinder. That thing was old as could be. I believe it was like probably 30 years old. Papa Isaac bought it years ago for probably $1,000. In that time, that was probably like $20,000 in our money. It was a very nice feed grinder. It was very old.

Times got better on the dairy farm, so they bought a brand new one, a New Holland if I remember right. They took that other one, and they were going to just junk it. Now, I'm not much on junking stuff. I like to think we ought to sell it and get some money out of whatever we can.

Well, they had a friend named Wiley Yarbrough. He gave that feed mill to Wiley Yarbrough, which was a nice thing to do. Wiley needed it. He used it for a little bit, and then it sat in the woods. Wiley got done with it and just parked it over in the woods and left it there and didn't care anymore about it.

Well, when I started with those hogs, we needed a feed grinder. Andy started talking about how we could get the money to buy one. A lot of times, those ideas involved Jay saving enough money from his job to buy one, and I was real careful with my money, believe it or not.

Grandma will laugh at this because I'm usually not very careful. Over the years, I've gotten worse with it. Now I'm getting better as I get older. I was very careful then with it. I thought, you know, I can go get that feed mill out of those woods. It was still working. It would just need a little bit of work, and I could use it. Andy said that thing's a piece of junk. It's shot. It was shot when Wiley got it.

Well, I didn't so much agree with that, so I went down there one day in my car. That's another story, what kind of car I drove. I think I had an old VW bug at that time. I loved that little car.

Anyhow, I went down there and that feed mill, it looked like it was fine to me. The tires needed airing up. It had a few pieces of metal that were rusted through, but I thought I could take some aluminum flashing from the store and wrap it around there and make that thing work. I knew it wouldn't be up to standards Andy had or a lot of other people, but it would work for Jay.

I went down one day with the tractor. It's about a 25-mile ride, a long way on a tractor that goes 20 miles an hour. It takes you a little over an hour. This is why math is so important because a lot of people think that's too far to go. Well, you do the math. It's 25 miles. A tractor goes 20 miles an hour, so every hour, you'll go 20 miles. Then you got five more to go, so five is 1/4 of 20, so that's 1/4 of an hour, which would be 15 minutes, so in an hour and 15 minutes, you can be from our house in Mitchell to where that feed mill was in Davisboro.

Now, that didn't seem bad to me. What's an hour and 15 minutes? Sometimes, we wait in line that long. I just did the other weekend at Universal Studios with all our crew at the Ace show. We went there for the evening, and we stood in line for an hour and a half. It wasn't even worth it. To a young fellow 17 years old, riding an hour and 15 minutes on a tractor? It wasn't bad. After all, I did something way longer than that one time with a tractor. I'll tell you that in another story if I remember it.

There I went on that tractor, and I drove down there. Course, I'd do this without telling Andy because he didn't think much of my idea. Sometimes people don't think much of your ideas. It can be kind of embarrassing to go ahead and do them. It kind of gets back into peer pressure, but you got to remember, if you have a vision, you have a dream, follow that dream. That's what I did. I jumped on that tractor. I was following my dream.

I went down there, and I hooked up that thing. I took an air tank with me. I think I might've gone the day before and aired up the tires. Nowadays, I probably would've realized that might not work, but it worked.

I think sometimes, when you have a dream, God knows your dream. He wants to help you. He makes things work for you. I don't think that. I know that. He's made a lot of dreams work for me in life.

Anyhow, I went down there and hooked the tractor up to that thing. It took a little bit. It was kind of stove up, like Charlie, my driver, says. It'd been sitting there for a while. I took a grease gun with me, and I greased it up so it would drive better, so the wheels would turn better and all like that. I took it easy. I didn't drive 20 miles an hour back to Mitchell. I drove about 10 miles an hour, which made it take about two-and-a-half hours home.

That was okay. I was saving lots of money here, so I was making a lot of money for my time. I drove those two-and-a-half hours. I got it home. It made it. Andy, he couldn't believe it. It actually kind of made him happy to see the thing resurrected, but he still didn't think I could get it running.

Well, I hooked up the power takeoff shaft to a tractor, and I suppose a lot of other people who are a lot more mechanical than I am (I'm not real mechanical), they would've taken it apart and did a lot of stuff to it before they tried to use it. I remember Andy saying what all I should do to it. Well, that was all French to me.

I didn't know how to do mechanical stuff. I still don't. I'm not a real mechanical person. I do understand a little bit about mechanics. It's important that you understand things. You don't have to know how to do it, but if you have an understanding of it, it gets you a long ways in life.

I didn't do all the things he thought I should do, like take it apart and put new bearings in and check it over and all like that. No, your hyper grandpa, who's a hyper 17-year-old teenager at the time, hooked it up to the tractor, to the PTO. That's the power takeoff shaft. That's what PTO stands for. It hooks to the tractor, and it makes things go.

I fired it up, and dust went to flying. It went to screaming. It grumbled, groaned, and moaned. And it eventually was humming like it always did. I worked at Avera Hardware back then. I brought me about $5 worth of aluminum flashing, screws, and bungee cords. Back then, zip ties weren't as common. I would've used them if I'd thought about it. I think actually I used bailing wire, like small, thin wire.

I wrapped it around the rusted tubes, and I made that thing work. I ground feed with it. I didn't have to go spend $2000 on a used one that he had found, $1500 on one that might work, that might need some help, or $5000 for a new one. For $5 worth of metal and a little bit of time, I had a real nice working feed mill.

I used that feed mill for about two years. Then I took that with me after I got married because Andy thought it was a piece of junk. Years later, after grandma and I were married, and Jeremy was a little boy, and we had hogs, I used that feed mill again. Then I sold it one day, I think for about $400 or $500, so there you go.

Now, once again, I didn't get very far in the hog story, but we're going to stop here. We're going to learn from this lesson that you can follow your dreams and you might save yourself a lot of money. You might accomplish something people say you can't do.

One man's junk is another man's treasure. I didn't make that saying up. Somebody else did, but it's very true.

Think about that, and don't be discouraged whenever you think you can make something work. Now, it may not work, but it might work. Some things I've done haven't worked, but I really can't remember very many of those. I can sure tell you about a lot of them that did.

Would you go get the Bear Cat feed mill if it were you?

*Good night! Grandpa*

# 27

## *The Hog Story*

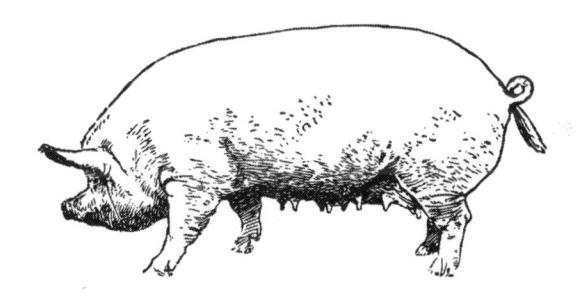

Well, I am still trying to tell the hog story. I want to tell you a real quick one before I get into that. We may never get to these hogs.

There's a lot of ways to tell stories. Ideally, I would sit in front of you and tell every one of these stories, but time won't allow that because I'd have to be sitting right there. We spend a lot of time together, but not near enough, I think, and sure not enough for me to tell all these stories at one time or at different times. I wouldn't remember them all anyhow.

I decided to write these stories down for y'all so you'd have them. I like to write. I don't know how to type, so my style is I write them out longhand, which means cursive writing. I hope you all learn cursive writing. Right now, at this point in life, a lot of schools aren't teaching it, but I wish that you would all learn it. It's a very valuable thing to use. You can write fast with it and put your thoughts down.

Course, nowadays, I'm going to get to this in a minute, there are easier ways than that to tell stories, but there's nothing wrong with a nice, handwritten letter.

I am digressing again, but I'm going to tell this story because it comes to me. When your Aunt Merita went to teach school in Arizona at Prescott Valley, they needed a teacher for about a dozen students. It was a new small congregation, and she wanted to do that. She did a good job of it.

When Grandma and I took her out there and got her settled in and said goodbye, I said, "How do you want me to communicate with you now that you're living way out here? Do you want me to call you every day?" Cellphones weren't quite as handy as they are today. She had one, and I had one, but they weren't smart phones like we have today.

"Do you want me to text you?" There wasn't WhatsApp back then, or else we probably would've done that a lot. We did later on.

"Or do you want me to send you an email, or do you want me to use snail mail?" which means to mail something through the United States Postal Service, which is about the slowest way to communicate it is. I said that as a joke. We both laughed.

When we got done laughing, she said, "I want you to mail stuff to me snail mail. I think it's really cool to get letters in the mail."

I'm probably going to cry as I try to tell this part of the story. That's okay. It's okay to cry. My dad told me that once. I never forgot it. I'll tell you that. Somewhere recently, I read that tears are the language of the soul. I think that's true.

I decided to send her a card in the mail every day, so I wrote a little card out every day. Sometimes, I'd write a long story. "This is what my day was like. It was a lot of stress. This went wrong and that went wrong." Or I'd tell her, "This is a great day, and this went right, and that went right. Or I'd just write a note, "I love you and miss you. I hope you had a good day."

When I mailed her the first one, she was so excited. The second one, she was excited. Knowing her, on the 100th one, she was still excited because she lived life very excitedly. That's a great way to live your life.

Anyhow, I remember at her funeral, the people she lived with, Dean and Pam Wedel, told the story of how every day there'd be a card in the mail, and how she was always so delighted. I missed a day now and then. I won't tell you one went every day, but I tried to send one five days a week for almost a whole year. I remember going there to visit her and seeing all those cards on the door and on the wall. It made me laugh and smile at the same time and cry.

I'm crying a lot now trying to tell this story, so I'm going to have to stop right here and collect myself, and I'll continue in a minute.

Anyhow, it was really fun to write all those cards out, mail those out to her. I had a lot of fun doing that. It's a very, very good memory.

I got off topic there. My style of writing these stories is either to write them longhand or just recently, I came in contact with my good friend Joyce Beverly. She is helping put this whole storybook together. If it weren't for Joyce, there wouldn't be a storybook, so this is really exciting. That's a whole 'nother story how we got together on that. Maybe I'll put that in the foreword of this book.

Joyce said it's okay if I record these stories, and she'll type them out. I tried doing that once before, and it didn't work very good, but telling the story works really good and so with WhatsApp, I can simply WhatsApp these stories to my extra phone.

I always keep two phones because it helps me get more done in life. That's another story, too. What I do is send them to my other phone, and then I send them later on to Joyce, and she or her granddaughter type them out, and so now we have them to read. That is how I'm writing these stories.

It works really convenient because I don't like to drive, and this morning, I'm driving from Wrens to Lavonia to meet Preston for the day. I didn't want to get grandma out early driving because she has a full day ahead of her. Charlie, my driver, has other driving he needs to do today, so it wasn't convenient for him.

I like a little bit of quiet sometimes, so I said I'll just go myself and listen to some stuff while I'm driving or else I can do some of these stories. At this point, I spent the last 50 minutes recording stories, and I'll probably spend the next 50 doing it, so that's how these stories get recorded or get written.

Now, where was I when I got off on that topic? Hmm. I'll have to think about this for a minute. Oh yes, the pigs!

Anyhow, I was telling you about these pigs, so we had these gilts. That's what you call a young female hog that hasn't had pigs yet. Usually, a gilt would be like a teenage female in the pig world, a female hog that's about half-grown. Even a little pig is called a gilt. So, we had these gilts, and they weighed about a hundred pounds.

We would make feed for them, and they grew up about 200 pounds. Then you get a boar hog, which is a male hog. You put the male hog together with the gilts, and after a while, they'll have pigs. We won't get any deeper than that in our bedtime stories. Anyhow, then when the hog has pigs, she's a sow, like a mama hog's called a sow.

When they have pigs, they'd usually have from eight to 12 pigs. Sometimes, they'd have a few more, but usually, eight to 12 would be a litter. I can tell you this without looking that up because I spent many a day and many a night sitting up behind a sow waiting for her to have pigs.

The reason I did that is because they can have them on their own, but a lot of times, they'll have them all at once, one after the other. One pig comes out, then another pig, then another little piggy. Then there might be a few minutes, and then there's some more. In five or 10 minutes, or more. It takes a little bit, and then one might not come out right. He might come out upside down or backward or crooked or something like that. The hog may have trouble having them. That can be a real issue.

I won't get a lot deeper than that for a bedtime story either, but I will tell you this. When a mama cow has a calf, she can turn around and lick that calf off with her big, long tongue. Now, this sounds really gross but that's the way it is.

When a baby's born at the hospital or at home or wherever, somebody helps your mama when you are born. They take you, and they wipe you off. They clean you up and get you dried off because you're all wet and gooey. You come out that way because that's the way God designed it. That way, it works a lot better.

When these little pigs come out, a hog can't lick them off very good. They have teeth. A cow does, too, but just something about a hog. They really can't lick their pigs off very good, and so pigs don't stand a really good chance. That's why, I think, God has it that they have eight or 10 or 12 at a time, so at least four or five of them will live. I'm sure in the wild, that's what happens.

First of all, in the wild, they don't have quite that many because they don't get as good of feed, like with all the protein I talked about being mixed in the feed. They may have five to 10 or five to eight, but at least three or four of them live, and trust me, they add up really quick in the wild when they have them like that. They add up in the domestic, as they call it, real quick for you, too, if you look after them.

Of course, again, like I told you about me, I would want to manage what I had very well, so when I'd see the hog look like she's ready to have pigs, I'd go out there with her at night and watch her. I'd see her lay down and make her nest, or later on, we had these little buildings we built called farrowing huts. Farrowing is when they have the pigs, and so it's kind of like a birthing place.

You'd make these things out of plywood. They were A-frame things. Again, I made them very cheap. It's a design that we had seen. Andy and I kind of perfected it from there. Inside, it has a little room. You build some two-by-fours inside there so the pigs can crawl out of the way of the mama sow so they won't get stepped on.

The sow kind of goes up in there and lays down and has her pigs, or as the pigs are growing up, she lays down and the pigs can nurse and get their milk like your little kitties nurse on their mama. You've all seen that. It works the same way with pigs, just like that.

I would sit there. I'd get up in that farrowing hut or, later on, when I had hogs just on some land I was trying to clear out, I would find where they're building their nest. I'd go sit there behind them. I'd slide up in there real quietly and not make a lot of noise or anything. I'd talk to the hogs. I knew them well enough. They knew my voice, kind of like a shepherd with sheep. They were used to me, and I'd sit up in there.

Course, nowadays, you can listen to music with earbuds or something else and pass the time, but they didn't have earbuds back then, or earphones like they do now. Maybe they did, and I didn't want to spend the money on them. I can't remember.

All I know is that sometimes I had music going out there. I had a speaker hooked up to my car. I'd have it out there maybe a hundred yards away. I'd have music going, so I could hear it in the distance.

The hogs were used to that because a lot of times, I would do that, play music, and I'd be out there picking up sticks and stumps at night on some land we were clearing up, or I'd be building a fence or things like that that most people would never do in the dark. I'd have the headlights on and my music going. I'd be out there digging holes and building fences by the moonlight!

I'd sit out there with the music going maybe a long distance away so it wouldn't scare the hogs. I'd sit there when the pigs came out. I had me a towel there, and I'd wipe them off and dry them up and get them a good start in life.

They come with these little tusks. You've seen big tusks on a hog. Well, they start with little ones. I would have me a little pair of side cutter pliers, and I'd reach in there and cut those teeth out, taking the tusk out right away. There's one on each side. They kind of hurt the sow whenever they're nursing. They'll hurt you if they get grown, so I clip those tusk out right away when those pigs are born. They hardly even notice the pain right then.

I'd give them a shot. I'd have some vitamins there. I would give them a shot real quick to help them get going in life, kind of like you do a baby when it's born. I'd make sure they got up to their mama, so they got some milk, and they start growing.

If I didn't do that, if I wouldn't be there, I'd come out in the morning, and a hog would have 10 pigs. They'd all be nursing because they do this on their own. They would be kind of dried off, but there'd be two or three dead ones. If I did it like I did, there wouldn't be any dead ones. That was really nice, unless there'd be a runt once in a while or something like that.

It was a lot of fun. I enjoyed it a lot. I can't tell you how many times, how many batches of pigs I helped be born. I would venture to say it was probably around 200 or 300 in my life, probably more like 400 or 500, enough that telling you the story 45 years later seems like it was just yesterday. I think I could still do it, but I don't want to stay up all night watching pigs be born now. It'd probably be fun for y'all to do that, though, and very educational.

Then we feed these pigs out on feed. We made a little higher protein feed for them because they didn't eat as much. We'd grow them up to be about 40 or 50 pounds, and we'd take them and sell them.

Each pig would bring anywhere from $20 on a bad market. I've seen them bring a hundred dollars, too. If they brought a hundred, you did really good. At that rate, every batch of pigs brought you about $800, but whatever it was, it was still a lot better. Maybe it was like $500 average per batch of pigs.

We could probably do that and have about $200 in it, so we'd make some really good money. That's part of what we lived on, and with part of the money, we bought more hogs or some cows for that farm.

Renting the Hyatt place was really nice because we could have our little hog farm going there and then have our cows. Later on, we ended up with about 20 cows. That was exciting getting them going. Also, the deer hunting I did there was awesome.

All this was because a 17-year-old boy saw an ad in a paper and had the courage to follow that ad and talked his parents into going and looking at it. We had somewhere cheap and really cool to live.

I think, now that I think about it, our rent was like $125 a month. We had been renting a house for about $250 a month and that house was an old house. It was very hard to heat and cool, and so that made our light bill about $150 more a month than what our light bill was at the Hyatt Place. So we saved a lot of money, a couple of hundred dollars a month.

We had a really neat place to live that we could actually make money off of. We had somewhere to hunt, which was really cool because otherwise, we had to rent somewhere to hunt or get a friend to let us hunt on their place. We had all those benefits.

I lived there until I got married two years later. There's another funny story I should tell about grandma. It's kind of embarrassing to her. That'll be another story.

Later on, after I moved out, I think my mom and Andy and my sisters lived there for another couple of years, so it worked out really, really good.

Again, have the courage to follow your dreams and ideas. You never know what they might do for you.

*Good night.*
*Grandpa*

# 28

## *The Bear Sighting*

Now, I know you boys are getting to the age where you really like to hunt. And that's pretty exciting. I loved to hunt, especially when I was younger. I still enjoy it a lot, although I don't do it very much. Now, I do a little quail hunting, maybe once a year. And that's a lot of fun to me. And I do go deer hunting once or twice a year. Of course, I hope to do a little bit more of that with you boys as you're growing up.

But when I was young, I did a lot of hunting. You've heard me say that numerous times. When my mother married Andy, he moved us out in the country and introduced me to serious hunting. And, oh my goodness, did I have fun! We did quail hunting. We did deer hunting. I met Freddie Chapman. There's a whole bunch of stories I could tell about me and Freddie hunting. I think I could write an entire book about hunting stories without any problem at all.

Freddie and I, we had endless fun hunting together. We coon

hunted. We shot rabbits at night out of his Jeep, which is not legal. We did squirrel hunting, every kind of hunting you can imagine. But deer hunting was my favorite thing. I spent a lot of time deer hunting when I was younger.

Earlier, I told you about living on the Hyatt place there in Mitchell. It was about 900 acres we had there. It was a beautiful place set on the Ogeechee River. And I remember doing a lot of deer hunting on that property. And again, I could write a lot of stories just about hunting on that property there alone.

But I remember sitting in the deer stand on one end of the property where I had hardly ever hunted. And I looked over my shoulder and heard something coming through the woods, making a fair amount of noise. And all at once, I saw a bear!

Now, we hardly have any bears around here. It was my first bear sighting ever! And my only one hunting. I've seen some bears up in Canada when I was up there for Vacation Bible School. And that was cool. But here I was in Georgia, Glascock County, and I saw a bear. It was really cool!

No way I could get a shot off at it. It just came up right behind me, and I turned around and saw him just kinda going through the woods on all fours. And just as quick as I saw him, he was gone, again. Of course, hardly anybody would believe me. But that was okay. Because I knew what I'd seen.

About two weeks later, I think Freddie and I again were out night hunting, which is not something you should be doing. And we shot a deer. It was late at night, and we saw some people come driving by right after we shot it, so we decided to go back later in the morning and get it a few hours later.

When we went back, over half that deer was gone. Something had picked it up and eaten it right in one spot! Not like a bunch of coyotes would do, tearing it apart. And it sure wasn't a buzzard because it was during the night. We figured that bear came through there and found that deer.

Have you ever seen a bear out in the woods or anywhere else?

Bears are really cool, but you got to be careful. You don't want a bear chasing you or getting you. They can do a lot of damage.

*Okay. Sweet dreams about hunting tonight!*
*Grandpa*

*It's funny how one story leads to another. That's the way life is. Life is all about stories. You're writing the story with your life. You may think these are cool Grandpa's stories, but you each one of you have your own cool stories, too.*

# Acknowledgements

First and foremost, I thank God who created us, each one a unique individual, creative in our own way with our very own combination of talents, humor, wit, and charm. We are all created in His image. What a thought! Thank you, God, for making me "me."

A huge shout out to my dear wife Mary, the wind beneath my wings, my constant encourager to press on, to put my thoughts down on paper. Without you, Mary, I doubt I would have ever had the courage to do this project. And thank you for your financial talent for managing money so we could fund this. Thank you, Grandma Mary!

To my first audience, my dear grandchildren. Thank you for listening attentively and asking for these stories. Without you, there would be no need for this book!

Thank you to my kids for giving us grandkids to tell these stories to! It is so inspiring to watch the mini versions of you grow up and conquer life one step at a time!

A big thank you to my dear mother, Brenda Isaac, for all of her sacrifices throughout my life that helped create these stories.

How can I express my gratitude for all the many teachers I had in my educational journey? Their talents for helping me learn spelling, sentence structure, literary arts, essay creation, and all the rudimentary skills that made this so easy for me. I hope some of you somewhere see this and know who you are. Your impact on my life is huge. Thank you.

Kiddos, listen to your teachers. You never know how and where you will use what they teach you.

To all of you who are mentioned in these pages: my dear sisters, Beth Turner and Jerri Lynn Bender (*Mary Margaret and Andrea, I'll see you in another book*); my Dad, who I regret isn't here to see this; my stepfather, Andy Isaac; all of my grandparents; my many friends along life's way who helped create these experiences – I say "thank you" from the bottom of my heart.

My heart is also touched and inspired by the very special "grandchildren" who were divinely placed in my life to enrich my journey and keep me smiling in dark times: Kate Eva Collins, Amelia Phillips, Robbin Norton. Love you – Papa Jay.

Thank you, Rita Peaster, for all of your assistance over the years in turning my fast-paced cursive into typed words that others could read. Your work on the early compilation of these stories helped us get this to print in less than four months from launch. Thank you!

Finally, how do I say thank you enough to Joyce Beverly and her granddaughter, Kate Walker, for all of your hard work in taking my notes, typed and cursive, and endless audio files then turning these into something we can hold in our hands and share for many years to come! I am grateful for all you did and for your talents and inspiration in bringing this dream to a reality. Truly, God leads in ways we can hardly fathom.

## JAY BULLOCK

*May God be with you all, and may you know He is with you every step of the way!*

*– Jay*

# About the Editor

## *Joyce Beverly*

Joyce Beverly has been sharing peoples' stories for more than 40 years. Her own story and Jay's intersect in the early 1990s when she was publishing her hometown newspaper and Jay was opening a new hardware store across town. Back in the day, Joyce met with Jay regularly to help with his marketing needs. They learned a lot together.

Today, Joyce helps people write memoirs and publish their books. While on a writing retreat in her old stomping grounds, she ran into Jay at a local diner. This book you hold in your hands today is a result. Stay tuned. There's more to come.

# About the Author

## *Jay Bullock*

Jay Bullock is an innovative entrepreneur with a huge heart for people and ideas. His business ventures officially began at age 11 and have encompassed the five decades since.

Jay's life journey has led him to a lot of unique experiences and places, from selling candy on the school yard and mowing yards, to dairy farming, real estate, and 40 years of selling hardware. Why not add author to the list? When he's not on the phone selling stuff, helping folks, or telling stories, he's always ready to share an adventure or story with a friend or soon to be friend.